DISCIPLESHIP

GIVING GOD YOUR BEST

GREG LAURIE

HARVEST HOUSE PUBLISHERS
Eugene, Oregon 97402

DISCIPLESHIP: GIVING GOD YOUR BEST

Copyright © 1993 Harvest House Publishers
Eugene, Oregon 97402

Library of Congress Cataloging-in-Publication Data

Laurie, Greg.
    Discipleship : giving God your best / Greg Laurie.
      p.   cm.
    ISBN 1-56507-039-9
    1. Christian life—1960— . I. Title.
BV4501.2.L3574   1993
248.4—dc20   92-20897
                                                      CIP

Printed in the United States of America.

Contents

Introduction

The purpose of this book is to call us back to New Testament Christian living as Jesus taught it and as the early church lived it. It is my conviction that *every disciple is a believer but not every believer is a disciple*! Jesus clearly calls all believers to be disciples. When we fail to respond to His call, we fall short of His perfect will and miss out on living the Christian life as it was truly meant to be lived!

What we often hear as the gospel today is a watered-down version that pales to the gospel the early church proclaimed. In the same way, what we often perceive as the Christian life is in many ways not what the Bible really teaches.

In our age of personal rights and independent thinking, discipleship seems like a radical concept. But in the biblical sense *radical* Christian living is really *normal* Christian living. In the following chapters we will look at four basic building blocks that are essential to being a disciple of Jesus Christ in the 90's. Make no mistake about it. If we live this Christian life as Jesus taught it and as the early church lived it, we will enjoy life to its fullest as we walk in the center of the perfect will of God. So join me in this spiritual odyssey as we follow the words of Jesus concerning the life of a true disciple. My prayer is that you will not only learn these principles, but that you will also apply them. If you do this the world may never be the same.

I am indebted to G. Campbell Morgan and Dwight Pentecost for their books on the subject of discipleship.

—Greg Laurie

CHAPTER 1

What Is a Disciple?

I am the true vine, and My Father is the vinedresser. Every branch in Me that does not bear fruit He takes away; and every branch that bears fruit He prunes, that it may bear more fruit. You are already clean because of the word which I have spoken to you. Abide in Me, and I in you. As the branch cannot bear fruit of itself, unless it abides in the vine, neither can you, unless you abide in Me. I am the vine, you are the branches. He who abides in Me, and I in him, bears much fruit; for without Me you can do nothing. If anyone does not abide in Me, he is cast out as a branch and is withered; and they gather them and throw them into the fire, and they are burned. If you abide in Me, and My words abide in you, you will ask what you desire, and it shall be done for you. By this My Father is glorified, that you bear much fruit; so you will be My disciples.

John 15:1-8

*D*isciple! *What comes to mind when you hear that word? You may think of the 12* disciples who walked the dusty streets of Jerusalem and the Judean wilderness following Jesus Christ. Or perhaps the word evokes images of a very disciplined individual who follows something or someone devotedly. But do you think of yourself? Do you know what it means to be a disciple? Do you consider yourself a disciple of Jesus Christ?

I want to help you understand what discipleship as presented by Jesus Christ really is, so that you can implement it in your life by the help of God's Holy Spirit. True discipleship is getting back to the Christian life as it was meant to be lived. In one sense we might call it *radical Christian living*. When we compare it to the anemic substitute people often offer as the Christian life today, it most certainly is radical.

The first-century believers who followed Jesus fully were men and women who turned their world upside down. They lived the Christian life as it was presented to them personally by Jesus. We too can participate in this lifestyle. We must embrace discipleship just as Christ offered it, the disciples apprehended it, and the early church lived it!

As I mentioned in the introduction, *all disciples are believers but not all believers are disciples.* Anything short of discipleship is settling for less than what God desires. We need to ask ourselves if we are living the Christian life as it was meant to be lived.

Is your life challenging? Exciting? Does it have purpose and direction?

If words like "exciting" and "challenging" do not describe your walk with God, if your Christian experience is dull, unfulfilling, or even boring, then it is time to seriously examine the statements of Jesus concerning discipleship. After all, how can we expect to fulfill the great commission to go into all the world and make disciples if we don't even know what it is to be a disciple? As the saying goes, it takes one to make one.

For starters, let's examine what is meant by the word "disciple," and its root word, "discipline." These are words that many people recoil from because they don't want to discipline themselves or wait for what God wants to do in their lives. But growing as a disciple of Jesus Christ is a day-by-day process. Jesus said, "If anyone desires to come after Me, let him . . . take up his cross daily, and follow Me" (Luke 9:23).

There are no shortcuts to holiness. There is no secret I can reveal to you that will take the place of years of walking with God and being conformed to His image. We live in an age where technology has made it possible to get everything quickly. We have one-hour photo developing, instant replay, touch-tone phones and suntan parlors. Banks have automatic teller machines. And a truly modern home today may contain a microwave oven, a food processor, a spin dryer for lettuce, a shower radio, a personal computer, and a device that looks like a giant hair dryer for blowing leaves off your lawn! Toothpaste even comes in a pump container.

We simply don't want to make the time for certain things today. This impatience carries over into our spiritual lives as well. We tell God we're in a rush, and if He wants to communicate something to us, He had better take advantage of the opening we have in our schedule after lunch. The motto of many Christians today might as well be, "Make it quick, God; *fax* it to me."

If you really want to be a disciple, you may have to radically alter the way you think about your relationship with God. As we go through these steps to discipleship laid out by Jesus, I'm going to ask you to seriously consider them and, most importantly, apply them to your life.

Follow Me

To be a disciple is to be a follower of Jesus. In Mark 2:14, Jesus called out to Matthew, "Follow Me!" Understanding this phrase will help us to get a better picture of what it means to follow Christ. To follow Jesus means "to walk the same road," and implies that we are to continue in that walk. As Jesus' disciples we are to walk the same road with Him in a consistent, ongoing fashion.

The phrase "follow Me" may be better translated "follow *with* Me." In other words, Jesus promises to be our companion and our friend as we continually and consistently walk the same road with Him.

A Litmus Test
for Discipleship

The Gospel of John contains three important texts that will help us understand what it means to be a disciple. In these texts we find three evidences or results of discipleship. Let's examine each of them for a moment.

You will bear fruit. The first result is found in John 15:8, the cornerstone text for this chapter. In it Jesus says, "By this My Father is glorified, that you bear much fruit; so you will be My disciples."

If you are a true disciple, you will continue to bear fruit. This means your life will display practical results as you follow Jesus.

You will study and obey God's Word. The second characteristic of a disciple is found in John 8:31, where Jesus says, "If you abide [continue] in My word, you are My disciples indeed." Disciples of Jesus will be students of Scripture and will walk according to its teaching.

You will love one another. A third trademark of a disciple is found in John 13:35, where Jesus says, "By this all will know that you are My disciples, if you have love one for another."

As a true disciple, your life will not only be characterized by practical results and a hunger for Scripture, but you will also have love for others— especially those who are fellow Christians. Without all of these characteristics you cannot really claim to be His disciple.

A Life Worth Living

Have you ever wondered why God put you on this earth in the first place? Why were you created? What is your purpose in life?

Our primary purpose in life is to know and love God. The book of Revelation tells us that God created all things for His pleasure (Revelation 4:11). What a thought! God has called us, before everything else, to know Him personally and to walk with Him, with the beautiful byproduct of this being that it will bring Him pleasure. I'll let you in on a little secret: It will bring *you* pleasure as well.

Another insight into why we were created is given by Jesus in John 15:16: "You did not choose Me, but I chose you and appointed you that you should go and bear fruit, and that your fruit should remain." From this passage it is clear that as a result of knowing and loving God, we will then bear fruit—fruit that will last. But what exactly is this fruit that Jesus desires in our lives? Surely it is important that we know, since He places such a high premium on it.

We find the answer in Galatians 5:22, which says that the fruit of the Spirit is love, which then demonstrates itself through such attributes as joy, peace, and longsuffering. Bitterness, hatred, and animosity toward others will be replaced by the love of God, shed abroad in our hearts by the Holy Spirit.

Planting Deep Roots

How is it then that we bear the fruit of the Spirit in our lives? The key to bearing fruit and thus fulfilling one requirement of discipleship is given to us in John 15:4, which tells us quite plainly that we must *abide* in Him.

What does it mean to abide? The definition of abiding conveys "a permanence of position; one's dwelling place; holding and maintaining unbroken fellowship with another." It is much the same as following Christ: walking with Him as our Lord and our friend with consistency. But it takes the idea further. To abide means that we are sinking our roots into a love relationship with Jesus. It is not simply walking with and serving the Lord when it is easy, convenient, or popular. When we abide in Christ, we remain in fellowship with Him daily, regardless of outward circumstances or inner emotions.

It is interesting that Jesus uses the analogy of a vine to describe the importance of abiding. It causes us to think of vegetation that when planted draws its strength from the soil of the earth. If we were to uproot a tree and move it to another area, then after awhile uproot it again and move it to a different place, it's quite possible we would damage that tree. If we repeated the process over and over, the tree would most certainly die. Yet that is how many Christians try to live.

Some believers have never found a place of consistency in their walk with God. Often they are the ones who respond to invitations to receive Christ again and again. Their problem is that they *come* forward but they do not *go* forward. They find themselves in a continual cycle of making "commitments" to Christ, but quickly falling away when faced with the pressures and temptations of the real world.

Following his sin with Bathsheba, David said, "Create in me a clean heart, O God, and renew a right spirit within me" (Psalm 51:10 KJV). A "right spirit" could also be translated as a "consistent spirit." May God help us to consistently sink our roots deeply into a relationship with Jesus Christ and walk with Him.

Work or Worship?

Real spiritual growth comes only through discipline and perseverance. Unfortunately, we often substitute activity for fellowship with God. The gospel of Luke records that Jesus went to the home of Mary and Martha to have a meal with them. In the story, Martha desperately tried to prepare a feast fit for the King, but became whipped up into a complete frenzy in the process:

Now as they were going on their way, He Himself entered a certain village. And a certain woman named Martha welcomed Him as a guest into her home. And she also had a sister called Mary, who also having seated herself beside the Lord's feet, was listening to His words. But Martha was going around in circles, over occupied with preparing the meal. And bursting in upon Jesus she assumed a stance over Him and said, "Lord is it not a concern to you that my sister has let me down to be preparing the meal alone? Speak therefore to her at once that she take hold and do her part with me." And answering, the Lord said to her, "Martha, Martha. You are worried and excited about many things but of few things there is need, or of one, for Mary chose out for herself the good portion which is of such a nature that it shall not be hastily snatched away from her" (Luke 10:38-42).*

What a fascinating contrast we find in this passage of Scripture. On the one hand we see Martha "going around in circles" and "over occupied," while on the other hand we see Mary setting aside the cares of the world to sit at the feet of Jesus and drink in His every word. Mary is the picture of a disciple who has learned the importance of *listening*; Martha is the picture of many Christians today.

We can easily identify with Martha in our chaotic world. Like her, we are often faced with choosing between a special activity and setting aside time to

* Kenneth S. Wuest, trans., The New Testament: An Expanded Translation (Grand Rapids, MI: Wm. B. Eerdmans Pub. Co., 1961).

spend with God. And like her, when we fail to sit before the feet of Jesus we usually end up frustrated.

There is no doubt that Martha's intentions were good; however, she substituted work for worship. There is a time to be active in serving the Lord, but before we can effectively work for Him, we need to first learn to wait on Him. Before we can give out to others, we must take in for ourselves. Before we can disciple others, we ourselves must learn what it means to be a disciple. A disciple will always take time to sit at the feet of Jesus.

This story takes on greater significance when you think of a disciple as a learner, as one who comes to be taught. More than a student passively listening to a lecture, this picture conveys the idea that the one who is teaching possesses full knowledge, and the one who is listening is doing so intently, marking every inflection of the master's voice and holding an intense desire to apply what is learned. The teacher bends over his pupil while the pupil drinks in the teacher's every word.

The attitude of a real disciple would be similar to that of a man on a plane that is about to crash. That man would listen carefully and intently as the instructions were given on how to survive the crash, no doubt hanging on every word. If I were that man and the flight crew was telling me how to use a parachute, I would not be interested in the magazine I was just reading or the dinner menu. I would listen intently because my life depended on it. That is how Mary listened to Jesus, and that is how we should listen as well.

God is far more interested in our inspiration than our perspiration. Mary learned the secret of abiding.

We need to learn the same if we want to truly be His disciples.

Cultivation

In our pursuit to become disciples, we make decisions every day that will either encourage or discourage our spiritual growth. When we get up in the morning, it's either the newspaper or the Bible, and later in the day it might be a choice between going to church and going to the movies. In dealing with others, we choose to forgive or to harbor a grudge. We choose to pray or to worry. With each choice we will either progress or regress, advance or retreat in our quest to be His disciples.

It always amazes me to see how much care and cultivation it takes to make flowers grow. My wife loves to plant flowers. She spends hours pulling weeds, driving out snails, and feeding the soil. It is necessary for their growth. But have you ever noticed how quickly and easily weeds can sprout up and take over? It seems a weed can bloom in the middle of a street or crack in the sidewalk. Without any caretaker or special watering a weed does just fine. But the delicate, vulnerable flowers require constant attention.

That is a classic illustration of the contrast between the believer's new nature and his old nature. If we want to be closer to Christ and live a life that is pleasing to Him, we need to cultivate and nurture our new nature. The moment we stop strengthening and building up the new nature, the old one comes back to haunt us—just like that weed growing in the street. It takes very little encouragement for our old nature to cause us trouble. All we need to do is neglect the new nature. The Bible says,

"Walk in the Spirit, and you shall not fulfill the lust of the flesh" (Galatians 5:16).

These are disciplines that every believer must maintain if he wants to live this Christian life as it was meant to be lived. May the Lord help us to learn what it means to be His disciple.

CHAPTER 2

Are You His Disciple?

And great multitudes went with Him. And He turned and said to them, "If anyone comes to Me and does not hate his father and mother, wife and children, brothers and sisters, yes, and his own life also, he cannot be My disciple. And whoever does not bear his cross, and come after Me cannot be my disciple. For which of you, intending to build a tower, does not sit down first and count the cost, whether he has enough to finish it—lest, after he has laid the foundation, and is not able to finish it, all who see it begin to mock him, saying, 'This man began to build and was not able to finish.' Or what king, going to make war against another king, does not sit down first and consider whether he is able with ten thousand to meet him who comes against him with twenty thousand? Or else, while the other is still a great way off, he sends a delegation, and asks conditions of peace. So likewise, whoever of you does not forsake all that he has cannot be My disciple. Salt is good; but if the salt has lost its flavor, how shall it be seasoned? It is neither fit for the land nor for the dunghill, but men throw it out. He who has ears to hear, let him hear!"

Luke 14:25-35

*A*re you Jesus' disciple? What criterion must we meet, what conditions must be fulfilled to be rightfully called by that title? The answer to these questions is found in Luke 14:25-35, which you just read.

To fully understand why Jesus made the statements He did in this passage, we must first set the scene at this time in His ministry. Jesus was fast becoming the talk of the town, and immense crowds thronged around Him wherever He went. If you wanted to get near Jesus, you needed as much determination as blind Bartimaeus, who screamed out for Jesus, much to the dismay of the disciples. Or you needed the faith and persistence of the sick woman who reasoned that if she could just touch the Lord in some way, she would be healed. And so, reaching through the ever-present multitude, she touched the tip of Jesus' robe and was healed.

Clearly Jesus was greatly admired for His dramatic miracles and insightful teaching. He had become enormously popular among the common people of that time, elevating the outcasts of society and assuring them of God's love while repeatedly blasting the religious hypocrites of His day.

In fact, throughout history it is evident that Jesus has always been an admired figure. Even today, many people regard Him as a great moral teacher. Moreover, today there are still multitudes that claim to be followers of Jesus. Many of them are filling churches on Sunday mornings.

The pointed statement Jesus made in Luke 14 about forsaking all to follow Him was directed to the fascinated multitudes that crowded around Him when He walked this earth, but it is still relevant for those who crowd around the church today. For back then, even as today, Jesus saw a problem developing. He saw people who responded to only certain aspects of His message. He determined that it was time to clearly lay out the requirements of following Him.

In this passage, we do not hear Jesus calling people to a marginal belief in Him. He was looking for complete and total commitment. He was looking for people He could call *disciples*. And that is what Jesus Christ is still looking for today. He is not looking for people to be called Christian in name only; He is looking for those who will commit their lives to becoming disciples!

In this passage, Jesus lays out the cost of true discipleship to the fascinated multitude. These were perhaps the most solemn and searching words that ever fell from His lips. Three times in this short passage Jesus says that if you do not do these things, you "cannot be My disciple." These are absolute prerequisites. I might also point out this is the one and only time He explained the severity of His terms.

I think many of us are like the people who listened as Jesus spoke those words. In essence, Jesus is still asking us, "Will you step out from the multitude and be a disciple? Will you be more to Me than a fair-weather follower?" A fair-weather friend is someone who stands by when it's convenient to do so, but as soon as things get difficult, he is gone.

Jesus has many fair-weather followers today. They follow Him when it's convenient, socially or economically advantageous, or when they are in the mood. But when crisis, persecution, or difficulty hits, they throw in the towel and turn away.

Curious, Convinced, Committed

In his insightful book on discipleship, Dwight Pentecost writes about this idea of radical Christian living, or true discipleship. He sums it up in three simple words: curious, convinced, and committed.

Like the multitudes, when we first see or hear of Jesus Christ, we are curious. Listening to what He said, learning of His life and the miracles attributed to Him, and hearing what others say about Him are obvious attractions—just like they were when He walked this earth. But there comes a time when we step over the line of being curious to becoming convinced. I would venture to say that many who attend church today have never really crossed that line. They are curious, but nothing more. They are attracted to the message, they are attracted to the Christian life, but they are not fully convinced it is true.

These people are like the multitudes found following Jesus in the sixth chapter of John's Gospel, where we read of Jesus feeding the 5,000. After He did this miracle, His popularity soared. The word on the street might have been, "If you want a free meal, follow Jesus of Nazareth." There's no doubt that thousands came to hear Him speak, but many were probably there for their empty stomachs, not their empty hearts! They were interested in Jesus' message as long as it took care of their temporary needs and as long as it was convenient. This becomes clear as we see their response to His message. After Jesus gave a very difficult series of teachings on commitment and sacrifice, these "followers" were repulsed by it and turned away!

After they turned away, Jesus then said to His disciples, "Do you also want to go away?"

They responded, "Lord to whom shall we go? You have the words of eternal life. Also we have come to believe and know that You are the Christ, the Son of the living God" (John 6:67-69). The curious went home. The convinced stuck with Him.

Another illustration of a convinced disciple is found in the second chapter of John. It is the occasion where Jesus performed His first miracle, turning water into wine. Following the miracle we read, "This beginning of signs Jesus did in Cana of Galilee, and manifested His glory; and His disciples believed in Him" (John 2:11).

In other words, they had become convinced that He was an extraordinary person—perhaps even the Messiah. But something more needed to be developed in their belief. They needed to go from being convinced to being committed.

This important event in the lives of Jesus' disciples is recorded in Matthew 16:13. Jesus was at Caesarea Philippi when He asked the disciples, "Who do men say that I, the Son of Man, am?" Their response was that many thought Jesus to be John the Baptist, while others thought He might be Elijah or even Jeremiah. Then Jesus said, "Who do you say that I am?"

Up to this point, the answers He had heard were those of the curious. Then a convinced disciple stood up and made a step toward being committed. His name was Simon Peter, and he said, "You are the Christ, the Son of the living God." Peter had passed from being curious and convinced to being totally and completely committed.

Where do you stand? Are you merely curious? Or perhaps even convinced? Have you made that step of faith to being committed? You become a disciple in the biblical sense only when you are totally and completely committed to Jesus Christ and His Word.

Deny Self

In Luke 14:27, Jesus says, "Whoever does not bear his cross and come after Me cannot be My disciple." Also in Luke's Gospel He says, "If anyone desires to come after Me [that is, if anyone would be His disciple], let him deny himself [say 'no' to himself]), and take up his cross daily, and follow Me. For whoever desires to save his life will lose it, but whoever loses his life for My sake will save it" (9:23,24).

The first step to being a true disciple is to deny yourself and then take up the cross daily and follow Jesus Christ. This flies in the face of the love of self, commonly accepted today even in the church.

We hear so much about "self-worth," "self-image," and "self-esteem." Yet this shouldn't surprise us, for the Bible warns us that this narcissistic attitude will be prevalent in the days before Christ's return to the earth. The apostle Paul, writing to young Timothy, gave us this insight:

> But mark this: There will be terrible times in the last days. People will be *lovers of themselves*, lovers of money, boastful, proud, abusive, disobedient to their parents, ungrateful, unholy, without love, unforgiving, slanderous, without self-control, brutal, not lovers of the good, treacherous, rash, conceited, lovers

of pleasure rather than lovers of God—having a form of godliness but denying its power (2 Timothy 3:1 NIV, *emphasis added*).

What an accurate assessment of the times in which we are living! As we look at our nation today, we see a society that is coming apart at the seams, and we must realize that America's only hope is a nationwide revival.

God gives us His recipe for revival in 2 Chronicles 7:14: "If My people who are called by My name will humble themselves, and pray and seek My face, and turn from their wicked ways, then I will hear from heaven, and will forgive their sin and heal their land."

One of the first conditions we must meet to see our sins forgiven and our land healed is found in the beginning of this passage: "If my people... pray." The word "pray" is interesting. Of the 12 Hebrew words employed to express the single verb "to pray," the one used here means to "judge self habitually." Not "love self" or "esteem self" but "judge self," and that habitually!

This is exactly what Jesus means when He tells us to deny ourselves. Discipleship involves commitment, and as I mentioned earlier discipline is not a pleasant word to many of us, but it is essential to being a disciple of Jesus Christ. It requires setting aside our own aims, goals, ambitions, or desires in life. It involves giving up our own will and rights.

Jesus underscored this when He said, "So likewise, whoever of you does not forsake all that he has cannot be My disciple" (Luke 14:33). That does not mean that to live a radical Christian life one has to take a vow of poverty and give every possession away. Jesus meant that we are to surrender our claim to our possessions. In other words, we are not to be possessed by possessions.

The only obsession a disciple should have is for Jesus Christ. *He* must be the most important pursuit in our lives. He must be more important than our career or our personal happiness; in fact, we will never find personal happiness until we are fully committed to Christ. Personal happiness is a byproduct of knowing Him. The Bible says, "Happy are the people whose God is the Lord!" (Psalm 144:15).

The Cross

Jesus underscored the importance of commitment when he referred to the cross. The cross has lost most of its original meaning today. It is shrouded in religiosity. It has become a symbol of many things, from a religious icon to an ornate piece of jewelry studded in diamonds or pearls. Yet the real cross of history was a hated, despised symbol. It was the symbol of a very cruel death. The Romans reserved it for the lowest criminals. It was a form of torture and execution.

The modern equivalent might be the electric chair. Now, we don't see many diamond studded electric chairs hanging around people's necks, do we? Nor do we see a hangman's noose with pearls on it. They are symbols of death, symbols of shame. The cross was the same thing. When a man carried his cross on the streets of Jerusalem, it was well known that he was going to die very soon. The convicted criminal would be driven outside the city, nailed to that cross, and set up by the roadside where everybody coming in and out of the city would see him.

Jesus said, "If you want to be My disciple, take up your cross." Why did He use that illustration? Why would He pick that despicable symbol of torture and rejection to illustrate what it means to follow Him? Jesus intentionally used a radical symbol to get people's attention. That is why we should look at it in its original context.

What does it mean to bear the cross today? Often we hear people say they have a "cross" to bear. "My cross is my children," they will say. Or the children of that woman might say, "Our cross is our mother." They identify whatever problem or obstacle they have as their cross to bear.

But that is not what the cross means. The cross symbolizes one thing: dying to self. For disciples this means that wherever Jesus directs, we should be willing to go. Obviously, this is not an appealing message to many people. Satan made an accurate statement of humanity when he said, "All that a man has will he give for his life" (Job 2:4). In other words, Satan knows that when the chips are down people will give up everything to stay alive, to preserve themselves.

Jesus was definitely not advocating an "easy believism." Far too often we hear, "Just ask Jesus in your heart. He'll make you a happier person. Let God be your copilot." Sometimes people will even tell us that God will keep every believer in perfect health and make him or her wealthy to boot! I'm sorry, but that is not the Christianity of the New Testament.

While it is true that Jesus will make you a happier person and much more, God is not merely offering Himself as some celestial big brother or good buddy. The bottom line is that God is absolutely holy and perfect, and we have all horribly sinned against

Him. But God, in His great love, bridged the tremendous gap that sin produced and sent His own dear Son to die on the cross for us. To receive Him into our lives we must not only believe in Him, but we must also turn from our sin and follow Him as both our Lord and Savior.

General William Booth, founder of the Salvation Army, wrote of the dangers he saw facing the message of the gospel in the twentieth century. Among other things he saw a "gospel" that would present Christianity without Christ, forgiveness without repentance, salvation without regeneration, and heaven without hell. And isn't that what we often hear substituted for the true gospel today?

I like what Samuel Rutherford said about bearing the cross. He said, "The cross of Christ is the sweetest burden that I ever bore. It is a burden to me such as wings are to a bird or sails are to a ship to carry me forward to my harbor." Rutherford discovered what you, too, can know—that when you really die to yourself, you really find yourself. When you lay aside personal goals, desires and ambitions, that is when God will reveal the desires, ambitions, and goals that He has for you. That is what the apostle Paul meant when he said, "I have been crucified with Christ; it is no longer I who live, but Christ lives in me" (Galatians 2:20).

Are you bearing the cross right now and following Jesus? For some people it may mean the suffering of persecution. It may mean a major change in your lifestyle. It may cost you friends. To others it could even mean dying for the faith. Whatever the case, bearing the cross will affect and influence every aspect of your life.

Until we recognize that everything we have belongs to Jesus, we are not disciples. If we are aware of God's will for our lives, but unwilling to go in the direction God wants us to go, then we are not His disciples.

Are you His disciple today? Perhaps you are still just curious, or only slightly convinced. Maybe you are convinced but haven't overcome that final hurdle of commitment. Until you reach that point, you cannot truly be called His disciple.

A true disciple who desires to live a *radical* Christian life must anchor himself in Romans 12:1: "I beseech you therefore, brethren, by the mercies of God, that you present your bodies a living sacrifice, holy, acceptable to God, which is your reasonable service."

Paul's idea of discipleship is not just giving intellectual acknowledgment to Jesus as God; it includes obedience and sacrifice. In the chapters leading up to Romans 12, Paul had outlined all that God had done for us. Now he says, "In light of all this, I urge you, by the mercies of God, because of what He has done for you, to present yourself to Him as a living sacrifice."

In the Jewish wedding ceremony, the moment at which the father of the bride gave his daughter's hand to the bridegroom was called the presentation. In the same way, God wants us to present ourselves to Him.

Do you want to be more than just curious about Jesus? If so, there needs to be a commitment on your part. The requirements of discipleship are different than the requirements of salvation. To be a Christian, you need to believe in Him whom God has sent, and then you will receive eternal life through Jesus Christ our Lord. It is a gift. To be a disciple is to take up the cross daily and follow Him, making His will your will. It is a commitment.

As you are learning, every disciple is a Christian but not every Christian is a disciple. Do you want to be more than curious about Jesus—and more than convinced? Then commit your life to Him as a disciple and discover what *radical Christian living* is all about!

Perhaps these requirements seem too difficult for you right now. Remember, if God asks you to do something, He will give you the strength to do it. God's calling is God's enabling. In Philippians 2:13 we learn, "For it is God who works in you both to will and to do for His good pleasure."

That is our guarantee. God will be our enabler. It doesn't take great knowledge, it doesn't take great ability—it only takes your *availability*!

The Cost
of Discipleship

Now it happened as they journeyed on the road, that someone said to Him, "Lord, I will follow You wherever You go." And Jesus said to him, "Foxes have holes and birds of the air have nests, but the Son of Man has nowhere to lay His head." Then He said to another, "Follow Me." But he said, "Lord, let me first go and bury my father." Jesus said to him, "Let the dead bury their own dead, but you go and preach the kingdom of God." And another also said, "Lord, I will follow You, but let me first go and bid them farewell who are at my house." But Jesus said to him, "No one, having put his hand to the plow, and looking back, is fit for the kingdom of God."

Luke 9:57-62

*I*f as a Christian you have gone from being curious, to being convinced, to making a commitment to be a disciple, there is still one other factor
that you must consider: the *cost.*

Obedience to God's plan of discipleship will definitely be costly. Too often, a would-be disciple
desires God's best, but fails to pay the price to attain
it! How can we be willing to give so little to the One
who gave so much for us? He gave everything to us
and He expects nothing less in return.

I'm reminded of the farmer who was known for
his stingy ways. This farmer happened to own a
cow. It seems that this cow gave birth to two calves.
The farmer looked at the calves and said, "Lord I'm
so thankful for this blessing that I'm going to give
You one of my calves."

He proudly told his wife of his decision, which
surprised her in light of his normally selfish ways.
When pressed as to what calf he would give to the
Lord, he replied, "I'm not sure yet."

Time went by, and after a few weeks one of the
calves began to get sick. After a few more days, the
farmer came in to the house from the barn with the
lifeless calf draped over his arms and very sadly
said to his wife, "Honey, I've got bad news. The
Lord's calf just died."

Many believers are just like that farmer in their
relationship with Jesus Christ. They give Him what
they no longer want, and God ends up with left-
overs! That is not the attitude we should have. He

35

has given so much to us that we should want to give everything we have back to Him.

He Must Be Lord of All

In Luke 9, Jesus gives a call to discipleship that underscores what obedience may potentially cost in our friendships and family relationships. Jesus called to a man, saying, "Follow Me." To that, the man responded, "Lord, let me first go and bury my father." A call to another man yielded a similar response, "Lord, let me first go and bid them farewell who are at my house" (Luke 9:57-62). Neither of these responses was appropriate.

We simply can't say, "Lord, let me first. . . ." If He is Lord, *He* must be first. If we come first in any way, then for all practical purposes He is not Lord in our lives. This same thing occurred to Simon Peter when in a vision a sheet was lowered from heaven with all kinds of nonkosher foods, foods a good Jewish boy would never eat. But God said, "Kill and eat." To which Peter replied, "Not so, Lord" (Acts 10:13,14).

Again, there is no such response as, "Not so, Lord." It is a contradiction. If we say no to God, it is an indication that He is not Lord. He may be a friend, He may be someone you look to with admiration, but He cannot be given a negative response by a true disciple. Either He is Lord of all or He is not Lord at all!

No Postponement

To the man who said, "Lord, let me first go and bury my father," Jesus said, "Let the dead bury their own dead."

Some people read that and think Jesus was being unnecessarily harsh. Actually, this was an expression used in the Hebrew culture that would have been readily understood at this time. The man was in fact asking if he could postpone his commitment. He wanted to wait until his father and mother grew old and eventually died. At that time it would be more convenient for him to follow Jesus.

Perhaps he was thinking, "Lord, if I go home right now to my mother and father and say I've found the Messiah and I'm going to follow Him, there are going to be problems and conflict, and I don't want that in my life right now. I have earthly relationships to which I am devoted. When things are more convenient, then I will follow You."

Jesus knows that being obedient in following Him will cause conflict. That is part of the price to be paid. We are either going to have harmony in our relationship with people and, as a result, friction in our relationship with the Lord, or we are going to have harmony in our relationship with the Lord and friction with people.

In other words, real discipleship, or, as we've called it, radical Christian living, will definitely cause friction in our relationships with nonbelievers. Even family members can be affected. If you want to get along with everybody, always make them happy, and never offend anyone but still want Jesus Christ to be Lord of your life and in total control, you'll find that it doesn't work. If you live a godly, holy life and let Christ be Lord of all, certain people are simply not going to like you. Sadly, some will even hate you.

Jesus told His disciples, " 'A servant is not greater than his master.' If they persecuted Me, they will also persecute you" (John 15:20). No one likes to have enemies, but as followers of Jesus we will have them. There are enemies of the cross of Christ, and because you are a follower of Jesus they will set themselves against you. And though it may be hard at times, we are called to love them.

The Scripture promises, "All who desire to live godly in Christ Jesus will suffer persecution" (2 Timothy 3:12). Now that is a promise I seldom hear being claimed by believers!

Jesus said, "Do not think that I came to bring peace on earth. I did not come to bring peace but a sword. For I have come to 'set a man against his father, a daughter against her mother, and a daughter-in-law against her mother-in-law.' And 'a man's foes will be those of his own household'" (Matthew 10:34-36). This often happens when other members of the family don't want to follow Christ as you have.

You might want to look at it this way: It's better to temporarily offend someone who doesn't know Jesus Christ with the convicting message of the gospel and see them ultimately come to faith than to never offend them in any way and see them go into a Christless eternity.

It's much like what a surgeon must do to save someone's life. He may have to cause temporary pain as he makes his incisions with his scalpel. Yet in the process he may prolong the years of that individual. Similarly, the message of the gospel may hurt at first as one realizes that he has sinned against God and must turn away from that sin. But it won't hurt nearly as much as what awaits those who have brazenly rejected the loving offer of forgiveness from the Son of God.

Unlimited Commitment

Another cost of discipleship gleaned from this passage deals with the extent of our commitment. Luke records, "It happened as they journeyed on the road, that someone said to Jesus, 'Lord, I will follow You wherever You go.'"

Surprisingly, Jesus responded rather coolly, saying, "Foxes have holes and birds of the air have nests, but the Son of Man has nowhere to lay His head."

In modern language Jesus was saying, "Look buddy, I'm not headed to the Jerusalem Hilton. You might want to reconsider. Mine is a life of difficulty and sacrifice. Do you know where I'm going? Ultimately I'm headed to die on the cross. Is that where you want to go? Consider what you're saying!"

We must give this man some credit. He was excited. He saw Jesus, admired Him, and immediately blurted out that he wanted to follow. He seemed to have a good heart, but he was impulsive. He had not first counted the cost. He did not know what was ahead. Jesus was making it clear that if this man was to be a disciple, he would have to forsake all that he had.

It's not any different for us. We must have the same attitude of detachment to anyone or anything that would slow us down. The Bible makes it clear that we are not our own. We have been bought with a price, and therefore we are to glorify God with everything we are. We recognize that we belong to Him, that our time is His time. Our life is His life. Our resources and possessions are His resources and possessions. We must consider all of this when committing to discipleship.

I'm told that in Africa, hunters have a remarkable way of catching monkeys. They take a coconut and hollow it out, cutting a little hole in it large enough for an extended monkey paw to reach into, but not large enough for a monkey to get his fist out. Next, they put some warm rice inside these hollow coconuts and place them under the trees, hanging nets overhead. Then the hunters go over the hill and wait.

When the monkeys smell the rice, they come down and reach inside the coconuts to grab the rice. The hunters have learned that the monkeys will not open their paw to let go of the rice, and therefore cannot get the coconut off. When they start banging the coconuts on the ground in greedy frustration, the hunters come and easily net the monkeys. Even as the monkeys see the nets, they still won't let go of the coconuts because they want the rice. As a result, they are easily trapped.

Many people live their whole lives for a handful of rice, a handful of possessions, a handful of pursuits. Like Esau, they sell everything for a bowl of stew (Genesis 25:29-34). They give up what God could do in their lives for fleeting, temporal things. True discipleship takes sacrifice.

I'm sure fewer people would get married if they adequately counted the cost. Courtship is often a dream world. A man takes his beloved to the finest restaurants, opens doors for her, and even brings her flowers. Then comes marriage. Afterward, there is still the dining out, only now it's at "take out" restaurants. And instead of presents, it's "Honey, will you sew this button on this shirt, wash these clothes, and have them ironed in 20 minutes? I'm going bowling." To the young woman's surprise, the prince of courtship has turned into a frog in marriage!

I'm not in any way demeaning marriage, for directed by the Lord with His principles at the center of it, marriage is a wonderful and fulfilling experience. But if it is rushed into without really counting the cost and following God's standards, it can quickly unravel. The same is true of our commitment to be a disciple of Christ. We must first count the cost.

Terms of Commitment

To count the cost is to understand the terms of the commitment. Jesus closes this passage in Luke by saying, "No man having put his hand to the plow and looking back is fit for the kingdom of God." That is a stern warning for those who wish to live a life of second guessing.

In a passage we looked at earlier Jesus used a military analogy to illustrate this concept. He said, "What king, going to make war against another king, does not sit down first and consider whether he is able with ten thousand to meet him who comes against him with twenty thousand?" (Luke 14:31).

Jesus was not necessarily implying that the king had only 10,000 troops available. It's quite possible that the king had 50,000 troops, but was only willing to commit 10,000 for battle!

In other words, Jesus would say to anyone considering discipleship, "I'm not asking if you are willing to commit 10 percent or 20 percent, or even 50 percent to Me. If you are not willing to commit everything to Me and recognize My absolute right over everything in your life, you cannot be My disciple."

How much are you willing to give? Is your commitment to discipleship like the story of the farmer and "the Lord's calf" that died? Or are you willing to pay the price and commit to radical Christian living? If you are, the world may never be the same!

CHAPTER 4

The Disciple in the Word

My son, if you receive my words, and treasure my commands within you, so that you incline your ear to wisdom, and apply your heart to understanding; yes, if you cry out for discernment, and lift up your voice for understanding, if you seek her as silver, and search for her as for hidden treasures; then you will understand the fear of the Lord, and find the knowledge of God. For the Lord gives wisdom; from His mouth come knowledge and understanding; He stores up sound wisdom for the upright; He is a shield to those who walk uprightly; He guards the paths of justice, and preserves the way of His saints. Then you will understand righteousness and justice, equity and every good path.

Proverbs 2:1-9

Having established what discipleship en-tails, *we can now examine some of the* building blocks essential to making radical Christian living a reality. The first of these building blocks is found in John 8:31, "If you abide in My word, you are My disciples indeed." If you and I want to truly be disciples of Jesus Christ, we must continue to be fed by the Word of God.

Why is it then that so many believers fail to read their Bibles regularly? A recent poll printed in *USA Today* revealed that of 662 people interviewed, 93 percent said they owned at least one Bible. But of that number, only 55 percent said they read their Bible. And of those who said they read, only 25 percent said they did so every day.

Yet, to a great measure, success or failure in the Christian life depends on how much of God's Word we get into our hearts and minds on a regular basis and how obedient we are to it. Everything we need to know about God is taught in the Bible. If we neglect the study of Scripture, our spiritual life will ultimately fall into disrepair.

Abraham Lincoln once said, "All the good from the Savior of the world is communicated through this book. All things that are desirable to man are contained in it." Honest Abe was exactly right!

Why is it, then, that so many believers fail to open their Bibles? Could it be that many Christians simply lack that spiritual hunger for the truth? One easy way for a doctor to know if a person is healthy or not is to check his appetite. When there isn't any appetite, it usually means something is wrong. In the same way, some Christians don't have an appetite for the Word of God. Some see reading God's Word as a duty, a bit of drudgery, an obligation. But that can change when we see the difference it makes in our daily lives.

Hungry children are healthy children. First Peter 2:2 says, "As newborn babes, desire the pure milk of the Word, that you may grow thereby." To desire the pure milk of the Word means that we intensely long for the teaching of the Word because we want to grow! If we are not making progress spiritually, it's very possible we are not yearning for the Scripture.

The prophet Hosea's cry is still relevant: "My people are destroyed for lack of knowledge" (Hosea 4:6). Today, many believers are throwing in the towel, falling into sin, or being misled by false teachings because they have never developed the vital discipline of getting into the Word on a regular basis. If we are to be disciples of Jesus Christ, leading effective and successful Christian lives, the Word of God must be a priority.

In Proverbs 2:1-9, the passage at the beginning of this chapter, there is a wonderful series of promises that will help us get the most from our study of Scripture. For every promise there is a condition that we must fulfill. The conditions listed in the first five verses state that we must receive His Words and treasure His commandments; cry out for discernment; and seek understanding as though we were mining for gold.

Receiving His Words

Let's examine the first principle of getting the

most from God's Word—receiving His word and treasuring His commandments (Proverbs 2:1).

What does this mean? Acts 17:11 referring to the believers in Berea, says, "Now the Bereans were of more noble character than the Thessalonians, for they received the message with great eagerness and examined the Scriptures every day to see if what Paul said was true" (NIV).

The Bereans were checking the accuracy of Paul's teaching against Scripture. If they checked out the apostle Paul, how much more should we be checking out our own pastors and teachers, and so-called modern apostles and prophets?

There are some people today who claim to speak for God. If anyone dares to challenge or question the validity of what they say, such a person is rebuked for daring to challenge the individual who claims to be a modern apostle or prophet. What foolishness! No person is above being questioned. If probably the greatest teacher the church has ever known was scrutinized according to Scripture, how much more those who often contradict it!

Together with a scrutiny of Scripture, the King James version says that the Bereans received the message with "readiness of mind." This was not simply an eagerness to learn something new, but a willingness to reinforce and apply what they already knew.

Many Christians think they know more than they really do. Often apparently mature believers are reduced to a blank stare when faced with a question concerning a basic Bible doctrine. They know what they are supposed to believe, but they can't defend it biblically. They believe it only because they've been told it is true!

This is very dangerous. We should never hinge our faith merely on what someone has said to us, no matter how credible and godly the source. If that person is saying something incorrect, our faith could be shattered. This is why we must base our faith solely on God's Word. We need to know it for ourselves!

Studying His Word

In 2 Timothy 2:15, we find these words: "Study to show thyself approved unto God, a workman that needeth not to be ashamed, rightly dividing the word of truth" (KJV). The word "study" means "make haste and exert yourself." The phrase "rightly dividing" means "dissecting correctly, cutting straight the word of truth."

Let me ask you some questions. Do you believe that Jesus Christ is God? That is an essential doctrine! Do you believe that Jesus Christ is the only way to the Father? Do you believe that God has a plan for your life and wants to reveal His will for you? If so, can you back your beliefs biblically? Unfortunately, many Christians can't answer these questions with intelligent, scriptural responses.

One reason for this is that often we do not read the Bible intelligently. Many times we read, but fail to understand what is being said in its context. We have no idea who is speaking and what the circumstances are surrounding the passage.

For instance, reading in the Old Testament about various animal sacrifices could be very confusing if I did not have a basic understanding of the New Testament. I might conclude that the best way to approach God is to sacrifice an animal. With an understanding of the New Testament, however, I realize that the sacrificial system was all foreshadowing what Jesus would do on the cross.

Here are some key questions you might ask yourself as you open the Bible and study a passage of Scripture:

- ✦ What is the main subject of the passage?
- ✦ Who are the people revealed in this passage?
- ✦ Who is speaking?
- ✦ About whom is that person speaking?
- ✦ What is the key verse?
- ✦ What does it teach me about Jesus?

As you read, it is also very important to ask how the text might apply to your daily living. When reading a passage, ask yourself these questions:

- ✦ Is there any sin mentioned in the passage that I need to confess or forsake?
- ✦ Is there a command given that I should obey?
- ✦ Is there a promise made that I can look to in my current circumstances?
- ✦ Is there a prayer given that I could pray?

Meditating on His Word

When you read the Bible, stop and think about what the Lord may be showing you. It's good to chew your spiritual food. That is what is meant by meditating on the Word. We are better off reading five verses slowly and understanding what they mean than reading five chapters quickly and not getting anything out of them. Learn to slow down.

Learn to meditate. Learn to allow the Holy Spirit to speak to you through each passage.

Psalm 1 gives us an example of a person who has learned to walk with God. That person is said to "meditate in His word day and night." We should do the same as His disciples.

Pray for Understanding

This brings us to another important ingredient in learning from Scripture. It is found in Proverbs 2:3: "Cry out for discernment, and lift up your voice for understanding."

The second step to getting the most from Scripture is to pray for understanding. Psalm 119:18 says, "Open my eyes, that I may see wondrous things from Your law."

We need to come before the Lord and say something like "Father, I believe You are the author of this Book. I believe as You say in Scripture that all Scripture is breathed by You. Therefore, I am asking You as the author of the Book to take me on a guided tour. Help me to understand, and show me how these truths apply in my life." That form of sincere prayer will cause the Bible to come alive in your time of study.

Treasuring His Word

The next principle is found in Proverbs 2:4: "If you seek her as silver, and search for her as for hidden treasures; then you will understand the fear of the Lord, and will find the knowledge of God."

If you want to know God, He tells us we should seek Him and His wisdom as though we were "mining for gold" or searching for treasures! Psalm

19:7-11 says, "The law of the Lord is perfect, converting the soul; the testimony of the Lord is sure, making wise the simple. . . . More to be desired are they than gold, yea, than much fine gold . . . and in keeping them is great reward."

Do we recognize what a treasure the Bible is to us as believers? Here in the United States, we've been spoiled in many ways. Many of us have more than one Bible at home. I have Bibles in different sizes, shapes, and translations. But in China today, and other countries where the Bible is restricted, it is a treasure. I've heard stories of believers in China who have only one Bible for an entire congregation. They take that Bible, tear out pages and give them to individual members of the congregation to memorize. To many Chinese Christians, Bibles are as valuable as gold—even more so. We need to see that same value in God's Word and not take it for granted.

Memorizing His Word

It is also very important to commit Scripture to memory. Many wonderful Bible memorization helps are available. Once Scripture is ingrained in your memory, it will always be there to use. There will be times when that verse or passage you memorized will pay great dividends. It will bring comfort to your heart, as well as needed strength in a time of intense temptation. We're told in Psalm 119:11, "Your word I have hidden in my heart, that I might not sin against You." Although it is good to carry a Bible in your briefcase, pocket, or purse, the best place to carry it is in your heart!

In Deuteronomy 11:18-20, God tells us, "Lay up these words of mine in your heart . . . teach them to your children . . . and you shall write them."

The best way for me to remember things is to write them down. When I write something down, it is engraved more deeply into my memory, much deeper than if I just read it. I might not even have to refer to what I wrote. Writing something down seems to help the material enter my mind and gives it more "staying power." It is a good practice to keep a journal or notebook with your Bible. When you study the Scripture personally and a passage speaks to you, write down what God has shown you. Maybe it won't be useful right at that moment, but the next day or a month later it may be just what you need.

Applying His Word

Finally, we must apply God's Word to our everyday actions and activities. As mentioned earlier, Jesus said that if we continue in His word, then we are His disciples. It's not enough to study the Scripture on a daily basis or even memorize it; it must affect the way that we live. It's not enough to go through the Word of God; the Word of God must go through you. It's not how you mark your Bible; it's how your Bible marks you!

The word "continue" is the same word Jesus used in John 15:7 when He spoke of "abiding." He said, "If you abide in Me, and My words abide in you, you will ask what you desire, and it shall be done for you."

We abide in Jesus as we draw strength and resources from Him. In the same way a vine draws its resources from the soil and the branch draws its resources from the vine, we are to maintain unbroken fellowship, communion, and friendship with God. If we are abiding in the Word, it means we are drawing our ideas and lifestyle from the Word. Consequently, our actions and speech are being affected.

Is the Word affecting you in that way today? Is it sustaining your life? Is it controlling your thoughts, the way you conduct your business, home life, and even your free time? If not, you are not a disciple. It is only when we put ourselves under the authority of His Word and submit to its teaching that we become disciples.

Colossians 3:16 says, "Let the word of Christ dwell in you richly." Another way to say this would be, "Let Christ's words be perfectly at home in you." God wants His Word to permeate every area of your life—your home, your business, your play time as well as your prayer time. Continuing in the Word is a necessity for all who wish to be His disciples.

CHAPTER 5

The Disciple in Prayer

And when you pray, you shall not be like the hypocrites. For they love to pray standing in the synagogues and on the corners of the streets, that they may be seen by men. Assuredly, I say to you, they have their reward. But you, when you pray, go into your room, and when you have shut your door, pray to your Father who is in the secret place; and your Father who sees in secret will reward you openly. But when you pray, do not use vain repetitions as the heathen do. For they think they will be heard for their many words. Therefore do not be like them. For your Father knows the things you have need of before you ask Him. In this manner, therefore, pray: Our Father in heaven, hallowed be Your name. Your kingdom come. Your will be done on earth as it is in heaven. Give us this day our daily bread. And forgive us our debts, as we forgive our debtors. And do not lead us into temptation, but deliver us from the evil one. For Yours is the kingdom and the power and the glory forever. Amen.

Matthew 6:5-13

*A*s we seek to be disciples, let us consider a second essential building block in addition to continuing in the Word. The disciple must be a person of prayer!

If we attempt to continue in the Word without prayer, our study of the Word is going to be merely an academic exercise. What's more, if we really desire to apply the building blocks of discipleship to our Christian life, prayer will be essential. Prayer is the key to having passion and power in our witness.

For a believer, prayer should be second nature, almost like breathing. But sadly, in the lives of many believers, prayer is greatly lacking. Perhaps this is true because many times when we pray, it seems like nothing happens.

When Job encountered his many trials, one thing he cried out was, "There is no daysman for me" (Job 9:33). What he meant was that he couldn't find anyone to reason or argue for him, no one who would stand in the gap for him before God. Job felt as though he couldn't get through to God.

Perhaps there have been times when you have felt this way. It seemed as though God wasn't really listening. If you have received Jesus Christ as your Lord and Savior, this simply should not be the case, for Jesus has paved the way for us to stand boldly at the throne of grace to find help in time of need (Hebrews 4:16). Today we can approach God through Jesus our Mediator. "For there is one God and one Mediator between God and men, the Man Christ

Jesus" (1 Timothy 2:5). We are also told in Hebrews 7:25 that Jesus "lives to make intercession" for us.

Motives for Prayer

As we look at this passage in Matthew 6, we find Jesus first deals with several common misconceptions that people have regarding prayer. The first misconception deals with motives. Jesus said, "When you pray, you shall not be like the hypocrites. They stand in the synagogues and on the corners of the streets, that they may be seen by men."

The problem with the "religious" people of that day, the Pharisees, was that they prayed to impress others. On street corners and in the marketplace they could be seen lifting up their hands and praying in a very ostentatious manner. Others would walk by and think, "Look at that man of God. He loves God so much that he can't even wait to get to the synagogue to pray."

What they didn't realize was that the person praying was most likely thinking, "What a man of God I am. Everyone is looking at me. Everyone is impressed with my spirituality. I am so holy."

That type of prayer won't be heard by God. A person so concerned with what others are thinking about him is too full of himself to be effective in his prayer. He is like the self-righteous Pharisee Jesus mentioned who "prayed thus with himself." God won't hear the prayer of a pride-filled person, for it is nothing less than sin, and the Bible tells us that if we regard iniquity in our hearts, the Lord will not hear us. Make no mistake about it—spiritual pride is every bit as much a sin as lying or immorality, even though it is a more subtle one.

Methods of Prayer

The second misconception about prayer that Jesus dealt with concerned *how* the Pharisees were praying. The Pharisees were caught up in repeating ritualized prayers over and over again. It seems they felt that the longer the prayer, the more spiritual and pleasing to God.

Prayer should come from the heart. God is not interested in eloquence. He is not interested in how perfectly our prayers sound, or if they rhyme, or how long they are. He is concerned with how genuine they are. One of the most eloquent prayers found in Scripture comes from a man who said, "God be merciful to me a sinner" (Luke 18:13). Now that's effective prayer! That is a man who is honest with God. He said what he was thinking and simply laid it out before the Lord. Sometimes we get so concerned with technique we completely miss the whole point of prayer.

When Jesus used the word "pray," he used a word that literally means to "wish forward." To "wish" describes a desire. It is a hope of our heart. "Forward" implies action. It is the idea of wishing something from the depth of the heart and bringing that desire forward to the throne of God. Often our mouths and minds can go through some ritualized prayer while our hearts never engage at all.

In Matthew 6:8, Jesus unmasks another common misconception of prayer. He says, "Your Father knows the things you have need of before you ask Him." God knows our needs before we ask! Prayer is not instructing or informing God. Nor is prayer bending the will of God. Some people think they can influence God or move God a certain way through prayer. Nothing could be further from the truth. True praying is not overcoming or changing God's reluctance; it's laying hold of His willingness. Prayer is not getting our will in heaven; it's getting God's will on earth. Martin Luther said, "By our praying we are instructing ourselves more than Him."

The Model Prayer

Now we come to the model prayer that we know as the Lord's Prayer. It probably should not be referred to as such, for it was not a prayer that Jesus prayed for Himself, but a model given to the disciples to teach *them* how to pray. Jesus himself never had to pray "Forgive us our debts as we forgive our debtors." He was sinless. This was a prayer for His disciples and for us. It might be more accurately called the Disciple's Prayer. And because this book is about discipleship, it is fitting we have a clearer understanding of this prayer.

Within this prayer, we are given the principles we need to understand how to communicate with God. The disciples had watched Jesus pray. They had seen Him spend time with His Father. They had seen His intimacy and His closeness with the Father. In contrast, they had also seen the ritualized, cold, academic prayers of the religious hypocrites. It was for this reason the disciples came to Jesus and said, "Lord, teach us to pray."

Jesus began by saying, "In this manner, therefore, pray." Let me emphasize that He was not giving them a canned, formalized prayer. In fact, this prayer was never repeated in the New Testament. That is not to say that it's wrong to pray this prayer or to use it as an act of worship to God. But it should not be adhered to merely as a ritual. There's nothing magical in simply uttering it. We can, however, learn from its form and structure how to pray more effectively. It is a model and pattern for all prayers.

This prayer is divided into two sections. The first three petitions focus on the glory of God, while the last three deal with the need of man. It should be pointed out that the prayer begins with "Our Father who art in heaven" and not with "Give us this day our daily bread." Too often we begin our prayers with our needs!

Getting Our Priorities Straight

When we pray, we should first recognize to *whom* we are speaking! It's good to pause before you speak in prayer and realize you are addressing the Creator of the entire universe. Too often we rush into the presence of God and absentmindedly rattle off our petitions. We ought to first be quiet and wait before the Lord before saying anything. Then, after a time of contemplation of whom we are speaking to, we will more reverently pray, "Our Father. . . ."

Those words should remind us that it is our Father, the One who has our best interests at heart, to whom we are speaking. We are told in 1 John 3:1, "Behold what manner of the love the Father has bestowed on us, that we should be called the children of God." From this we can be assured that whatever happens as a result, our prayer is in accordance with what our Father wants for us. We may not always agree with what He decides, but we can be assured that His will for us is good. We know He loves us with an everlasting love.

And when we pray to our Father in heaven, it should remind us that He is the Creator. That should fill our hearts with humility and awe. Just uttering those words helps to prepare our hearts, and to see our smallness in light of His greatness.

Hallowed Be Your Name

Next, the disciples' pattern of prayer brings us to the statement "hallowed be Your name." Following our acknowledgment of whom we are speaking to, the loving Father and Creator, we are then reminded of His holiness. That phrase "hallowed" could also be translated "sanctified, revered," or "holy" is His name. It recognizes that we should want to be sanctified or set apart for Jesus Christ to live holy lives. Because He is holy, so we should also live holy lives. All of our ambitions, interests, and pursuits should reveal that we follow a holy God.

A prayer that is powerful must be prayed for God's glory. When you read through the Scriptures, you will find that the great prayers recorded in the Bible always glorify God and set Him apart (such as Elijah's prayer on Mount Carmel).

We are told in James 4:3, "When you ask, you do not receive, because you ask with wrong motives, that you may spend what you get on your pleasures" (NIV). The privilege of prayer was not given to us so that we could demand things from God. We should ask for the things He wants to give us. If God gave us everything we asked for, it would ultimately destroy us. We must seek His glory more than our own desires.

I've found that when I seek God's glory, His will and His kingdom, He blesses me. It is not wrong to ask for what you believe is necessary, but I make it a point to preface my prayers with something like, "Lord, I think this would be a great thing for You to do and I really think You ought to do it, but Your will be done. If I am missing something, if there's more to this than I know, overrule my petition. I know whatever You do will be best." That is prayer with His glory in mind!

Your Kingdom Come

The next phrase in our model prayer is "Your kingdom come. Your will be done on earth, as it is in heaven." A person cannot pray "Your kingdom come" until he can first pray "My kingdom go." Often our prayers, for all practical purposes, are meant to establish *our* kingdom. We want to be the captain of our own ship, the master of our own destiny. This will not do if we truly want His kingdom and if we truly want to be His disciples. We must turn over the reins of leadership completely to Him.

Therefore, it is essential that we learn what the will of God is, so that we can pray for it. In 1 John 5:14,15 we find, "Now this is the confidence that we have in Him, that if we ask anything according to His will, He hears us. And if we know that He hears us, whatever we ask, we know that we have the petitions we have asked of Him."

If you pray according to the will of God, your prayers will always be answered in the affirmative. As Jesus put it in John 15:7, "If you abide in Me and My words abide in you, you will ask what you desire, and it shall be done for you." Literally, this verse means, "I command you to ask at once for yourselves whatever you desire and it's yours."

As we spend time in the Word of God as a disciple and learn the will of God and desires of God, our prayers will change. They will no longer be self-centered or self-indulgent. Instead, they will be oriented toward the glory and will of God. As we align ourselves with His will, and start praying for it, we will begin to see the results. Most prayers are not answered because they are outside the will of God.

Once we have discovered God's will, we can pray aggressively and confidently for it. We can pray believing it will happen because we know it is not something we've dreamed up. In James 1:6,7, we read that when we pray, we should "ask in faith, nothing wavering, for he that doubts is like a wave of the sea driven with the wind and tossed. For let not that man think that he shall receive anything from the Lord."

When Jesus went to His hometown, we are told that "He did not do many mighty works there because of their unbelief" (Matthew 13:58). In other words, unbelief will cancel our own prayers. We must pray believing.

Where do we get such faith? The Bible says, "Faith comes by hearing, and hearing by the word of God" (Romans 10:17). I can pray believing that God will save a person's soul because I'm told in Scripture that God is "not willing that any should perish but that all should come to repentance" (2 Peter 3:9). Therefore, I can pray believing and hoping that God will save that individual. Nevertheless, the ultimate result is God's doing, not my praying.

I can also pray with biblical authority for revival in our country, city, home, or church. I believe this is something God wants to do because as we have seen it is clearly proclaimed in Scripture (see 2 Chronicles 7:14). And on a more personal level, I can pray authoritatively that God would make me more like

Jesus, and that He would reveal His will to me (see Romans 8:29; 12:2). The Scripture clearly mandates many things that are the will of God.

Give Us This Day Our Daily Bread

After establishing to whom we are speaking and acknowledging His rightful position, we then come to the first petition, "Give us this day our daily bread."

Let me again emphasize the order of this model prayer that Jesus gave us, as disciples, to pray. The way some people pray today, you would think that Jesus said, "After this manner pray, Our Father who art in heaven, give us this day our daily bread. . . ." But God is not our heavenly butler. Before a word of personal petition is uttered, Jesus shows us that we must first realize who it is we are speaking to and ask for His will above our own.

Notice that the prayer does not say, "Give us this year our yearly bread" or even, "Give us this month our monthly bread." God wants us to rely on Him *daily*! Sadly, many people do not want to depend on God. They would rather depend on themselves.

It's noteworthy that Jesus described Himself as the bread of life. We must seek a fresh encounter each day with Jesus Christ as we partake of the living bread. Yesterday's bread is largely useless for today. It is much like the manna provided by God for the children of Israel in their wilderness wanderings. The manna would not keep overnight. It would putrefy. It was good for that day only.

In the same way, God wants to give you fresh direction each day. The Scripture tells us, "The steadfast love of the Lord is never ending. His mercies never come to an end. They are new every morning" (Lamentations 3:22,23). God wants to bring a newness in our relationship with Him as He works in our lives.

Forgive Us Our Debts

The second petition is "Forgive us our debts, as we forgive our debtors." A true disciple will recognize the need for confession of sin, because the Scriptures say that unconfessed sin will hinder prayer. As I already pointed out, the Bible tells us, "If I regard iniquity in my heart, the Lord will not hear" (Psalm 66:18). In other words, if I hold onto or cling to sin in my life, God will not hear me. We should always remember to ask God to forgive our sins, even those we are not aware of. After all, the only sin God cannot forgive is the one we will not confess.

Some people have misunderstood the second part of this phrase, "as we forgive our debtors." They teach that the condition of being forgiven is that I must first forgive others. I do not believe this because it is a clear contradiction to other scriptural teachings. The only basis for receiving forgiveness from God is asking for it: "If we confess our sins, He is faithful and just to forgive us our sins and to cleanse us from all unrighteousness" (1 John 1:9).

Clearly God does not make forgiveness a prerequisite for being forgiven. What He is saying is this: If you have really been forgiven, and you understand something of that forgiveness, you will be forgiving to other people. If you are not forgiving to other people, I question whether you know anything of God's forgiveness in your own life.

A forgiven person will be a forgiving person. A true disciple will harbor no grudge in his life toward another. The disciple knows it will hinder his prayer life and his walk with God. Let's not forget what Jesus said, "By this all will know that you are My disciples, if you have love for one another" (John 13:35).

For that reason, no child of God can walk around with bitterness, anger, or hostility in his heart toward another person without feeling the conviction of his sin. We must forgive others as we have been forgiven.

Deliver Us from Evil

Jesus concludes this prayer with, "Deliver us from the evil one. For Yours is the kingdom and the power and the glory forever." The "evil one" is an obvious reference to Satan. We are to recognize our total weakness apart from God and the fact that we are engaged in a spiritual battle. We need our Father's protection. Without Him we are completely vulnerable. We must be dependent upon Him for daily bread, dependent upon His will for direction, and dependent upon Him for power.

Finally, with this model prayer as our guide, we must not fail to "pray without ceasing" (1 Thessalonians 5:17). As we do this, these essential ingredients of effective prayer will help us make great strides in being disciples of Jesus!

CHAPTER 6

The Disciple in the Church

And they continued steadfastly in the apostles' doctrine and fellowship, in the breaking of bread, and in prayers. Then fear came upon every soul, and many wonders and signs were done through the apostles. Now all who believed were together, and had all things in common, and sold their possessions and goods, and divided them among all, as anyone had need. So continuing daily with one accord in the temple, and breaking bread from house to house, they ate their food with gladness and simplicity of heart, praising God and having favor with all the people. And the Lord added to the church daily those who were being saved.

Acts 2:42-47

*S*o far, we have seen two essential building blocks in our growth as disciples of Jesus Christ: diligent study of and obedience to the Word of God, and consistent prayer.

The third building block for what we've been calling "radical Christian living" has to do with the significance of the church in the life of the disciple. Regular fellowship and participation in the church for a disciple cannot be overemphasized. As we come into the church and find our place in it, we are then in a position to give to others what God has given to us. Every Christian has an important part to play in the body of Christ, and to each one, God has given special gifts.

In Hebrews 10:24,25, we are given a key Scripture: "Let us consider one another in order to stir up love and good works, not forsaking the assembling of ourselves together, as is the manner of some, but exhorting one another, and so much the more as you see the Day [of the Lord] approaching."

Notice the emphasis is not on what a believer gets from the church, but on what he can contribute. The church is not only a place where we can come and be taught the Word of God and worship Him; it is also a place where we can come to be equipped for service.

A healthy church will be filled with believers who desire not only to get, but to give. Rather than having an attitude of "bless me, feed me, do something for me," their attitude will be "I want to help out. I want to follow the example of Jesus, who came not to be ministered to, but to minister."

That is not to say that believers do not need to be ministered to and spiritually nourished when we go to church, but we should recognize our privilege and responsibility to give out as well. We will discuss this more fully in a later chapter. For now the important thing to remember is that if a need arises or an opportunity comes to serve God, we should be willing to leave our seat in the nice, warm church and volunteer. The right attitude of a truly thankful Christian is "God has given to me and, as a result, I want to give to others."

Many people have become passive spectators in the church, charter members of the "bless me club." This mentality causes spiritual stagnation. Christians who have known the Lord for many years and have regularly attended church and Bible studies can stagnate if they take part only in the activities that benefit them. God did not intend for us to take in without ever giving anything out.

Secrets of the Early Church

To better understand how we should function as disciples in the church, we need to look at the New Testament church as Jesus established. The second chapter of Acts, which you read at the beginning of this chapter, records the first day in the life of the church. Here we find the first-century disciples in action. We also find principles that make for an effective church and for the true disciple's place in it.*

---

* My book *On Fire* (Harvest House, 1992) examines what made the early church so effective in turning their world upside down for Jesus Christ. I would encourage you to read it, for it picks up where this book leaves off.

A first glance at this passage reveals that the early church was dramatically different from much of the church today. What was normal to them is radical to us. That is why we have termed discipleship "radical Christian living." Normal Christian living as presented in the New Testament was a passionate, Spirit-empowered, all-consuming devotion to God and to His Word.

Power for Living

We must always remember that the early church was set into motion by the Holy Spirit. To be effective Christians, we must also be dependent upon the power of the Holy Spirit. There is a dimension of power that is available for every believer beyond the conversion experience. When we become Christians, the Holy Spirit takes up residence inside of us. He is there to guide us into all truth. He is there to seal us with His assurance that we are children of God.

But then there is another dimension of power available to us as believers. In the first chapter of Acts, Jesus said to His disciples, "You shall receive power when the Holy Spirit has come upon you; and you shall be witnesses to Me." The word that Jesus used there for "upon" is a different word than that which is used elsewhere when speaking of the Spirit coming inside of us. This experience is an empowering that gives us the boldness we need to live the Christian life. It is not an empowering to do "spiritual calisthenics," nor is it an excuse for hyperemotionalism. It is the power to live a consistent life, the power to be bold enough to share your faith.

The early church began in the power of the Spirit and continued that way. If we want to flourish and be effective in our witness for Jesus Christ as Christians, we must begin in the power of the Spirit and stay dependent upon that power until our last day.

The first ingredient that made the early disciples effective is found in Acts 2:42: "They continued steadfastly in the apostles' doctrine and fellowship, in breaking of bread, and in prayers."

Continued Steadfastly

These early believers had an intense passion to participate in the life of the church. And not only was there passion behind their action, but there was a consistency, a steadfastness. Passion and consistency were the keys to helping them do God's will.

The early believers did not take for granted the privilege of meeting together. The more I travel, the more thankful I have become for what God is doing here in our country in our own churches. Pastors from Yugoslavia have told me how hard it is to do what God wants them to do with the restrictions imposed by their government. Pastors in Ethiopia, some of whom had been in prison for preaching the Gospel, have told me how they and members of their congregations have been tortured and imprisoned for following Jesus. We are privileged here in the United States to have the freedoms we do. We must never take them for granted, and we must remember to keep our brothers and sisters who live in restricted countries in prayer.

What is your attitude toward going to church? As mentioned earlier, 1 Peter 2:2 says, "As newborn babes, desire the pure milk of the word, that you may grow thereby."

When you go to church, do you go with that earnest hunger for the spiritual milk of the Word? Do you crave it? That passion can certainly make a difference.

Where was this passion of the early believers directed? It was directed toward the apostles' doctrine! We have already pointed out how important the study of the Word of God is. The early church continued in the Word of God. As disciples, we must do the same.

Fellowship

We also read that their passion was directed toward fellowship. Today we have somehow lost the real meaning of this word. Often we hear it used at church gatherings, where there is to be "food, fun, and fellowship." But is that what the early church was experiencing? What is fellowship, exactly?

First of all, fellowship is not merely Christian social activity. Though it may involve that to some extent, true fellowship encompasses a much greater commitment. The word that is used for fellowship in the Scripture is a very distinct word. It's the Greek word *koinonia*, a word full of meaning, that can also be translated "communion," "distribution," "contribution," "partnership," and "partakership." Every one of those words provides a different facet of this word.

In part, fellowship is a common link with another individual that includes friendship, spiritual intimacy, unity, and a partnership in doing the work of Christ here on earth.

The word communion speaks of that friendship and intimacy. God wants us to have friendship and intimacy not only with Him, but with one another. It is a bond that can bring Christians together like no other bond, even closer than the bond of a family. Two believers share a unique exchange as God's Spirit works in their lives.

Then there is the word partnership, which implies cooperation. Fellowship is not only mystical communion; it's also practical. It involves helping and working with another person, as well as praying for and worshiping with that individual.

Finally, there are the elements of contribution and distribution. These also imply practical help for fellow believers through the sharing of food, clothing and other needs. In James 2:15,16 we are told that if we see brothers and sisters destitute and in need and fail to help them we are without faith! When confronted with such a situation, we need to obey God and help these fellow Christians. That is fellowship. We see this element of fellowship clearly at work in the early church as we read that they shared "all things in common."

God delights in His people gathering together for *koinonia* fellowship. In fact, God promised to manifest Himself uniquely at these times. He told Israel that He "dwelt within the praises of His people." This is true as we have times of worship and praise together. When we, with other believers, set our eyes and hearts above our circumstances and focus upon our Father, it brings everything else into perspective. God's presence is uniquely sensed at those times.

God will even manifest Himself in a special way in our conversations with other Christians. In Malachi 3:16, we find, "Those who feared the Lord talked with each other, and the Lord listened and heard. A scroll of remembrance was written in his presence concerning those who feared the Lord and honored his name" (NIV). In its original Hebrew the phrase "the Lord listened and heard" conveys a moving word picture. It means "to prick the ear; to bend down so as not to miss a word."

In essence, God is saying, "When My people come together and speak of Me, it pricks My ear. It causes Me to come down and listen carefully so as to not miss a word." That is both exciting and frightening. You've heard it said that Jesus is the unseen listener to every conversation. Think about that! When Jesus hears us mention His name to our fellow Christians, it's as though He says, "Oh, they're talking about Me. I want to hear."

If that's not enough, there is also a scroll of remembrance written in His presence containing the names of all those who fear the Lord and honor His name in true biblical fellowship!

Along with fellowship, the early Christians also "continued in prayers." The word "prayer" could also be translated "steadfast earnestness." As we pointed out in the last chapter, prayer is not only a key element in being a disciple of Jesus, it is a primary element of an effective church. The early church was characterized by steadfast, earnest prayer.

Gladness and Singleness of Heart

The first disciples in the church had a "gladness and singleness of heart." Are you glad when it's time to get up in the morning and go to church? David said, "I was glad when they said to me, 'Let us go into the house of the Lord'" (Psalm 122:1). These days (particularly on a Super Bowl Sunday) some might say, "I was mad when they said unto me, 'Let us go into the house of the Lord'"!

Isn't it interesting how arguments start on Sunday mornings over going to church, especially when there's someplace else to go? We will make up a host of excuses as to why we can't go on that particular Sunday: "It looks like it might rain today," or "It's too crowded." Yet we wouldn't think twice about going to a mall on a rainy day, even if we had to park a mile from the entrance. It's all a matter of priorities, isn't it?

I've heard it said, "An excuse is the skin of reason stuffed with a lie." The early believers, however, didn't appear to have excuses. Instead, they had "singleness of heart." Their lives had one purpose and were pointed in one direction.

When addressing His disciples in the Sermon on the Mount, Jesus said, "If therefore your eye is good, your whole body will be full of light, but if your eye is bad your whole body will be full of darkness" (Matthew 6:22,23). If we are set apart for God and His singular purpose, we will be seeking Him first and our lives will be full of light. On the other hand, if we have an eye that is dark, that means we have double vision. Though we may be looking to the Lord, we are also looking to the world. When we try to pursue both what God and the world have to offer, our lives will be full of darkness and confusion.

The early church focused on what was important, and they let nothing get in the way. If we allow ourselves to be fed from the things of this world, it will dull our appetite for the Word and pull us away from the Lord. This will lessen our interest in prayer and our desire to be with God's people. But when we are living as disciples, we will look forward to

Sunday worship, as well as other midweek opportunities. Meeting with other believers will be like a spiritual oasis where we can be refreshed. It will be an occasion to encourage one another as we go out to live in this world as witnesses for Jesus Christ.

Growing in Jesus

Finally, we read that the Lord "added to the church daily those who were being saved." A healthy church is a growing church. In the same way, a healthy believer is one who will be a shining light in this world of darkness. And even as the Lord adds to the church daily, a disciple of Jesus will be an instrument of God, drawing people to Christ by doing his part within the church.

CHAPTER 7

The Discipling of Others

All authority has been given to Me in heaven and on earth. Go therefore and make disciples of all the nations, baptizing them in the name of the Father and of the Son and of the Holy Spirit, teaching them to observe all things that I have commanded you; and lo, I am with you always, even to the end of the age.

Matthew 28:18-20

We now come to the practical result of being a disciple of Jesus Christ—passing on what we have learned and discipling others. Jesus gave us our marching orders prior to His ascension. To feel the impact these orders are to have on our lives as His disciples, we must make two important observations.

First, the three verses you just read are often referred to as the "great commission." Notice that it is a *commission* as opposed to a *suggestion*. Jesus never suggested that we His followers carry the gospel to the world. It was, and *is*, a command!

Second, these words were not directed merely to the original 12 disciples, nor are they meant for only pastors, evangelists, and missionaries. They are for every follower and disciple of Jesus Christ. If I am His disciple, I am commanded to go and make disciples of others. If I am not making disciples of others, I'm not really being the disciple He wants me to be!

What then does it mean to make disciples? Verse 20 defines it as "teaching them to observe all things that I have commanded you." Simply put, it is not only sharing our faith with others, but living out our faith so that people may observe it in action— teaching the gospel message by word and modeling it by example. With that understanding, we have a proper basis for examining in greater detail what it means to "disciple" another individual.

How to Effectively
Share Your Faith

Let me emphasize that God will never ask us to do anything that He will not give us the power to do. The calling of God is the enabling of God (see 2 Corinthians 3: 4-6). If He has commanded us to go out and make disciples, we can be confident that He will be there to give us the ability to see it through.

Notice He said, "All authority has been given to Me in heaven and on earth. Go therefore and make disciples." What is the connection? If the power is in Him and He is living inside us, then His power and resources are at our disposal to accomplish this task!

We all need to ask God for a strong dose of boldness from His Holy Spirit. We see an interesting display of this boldness in the lives of Peter and John in Acts 4:23-31. Peter and John had been preaching the gospel, infuriating the religious leaders of that time. As a result they were arrested and forbidden to ever preach again. They couldn't comply with that, so they prayed, "Now, Lord, look on their threats, and grant to Your servants that with all boldness they may speak Your word." After they prayed, the place where they were meeting was shaken, and they were filled with the Holy Spirit and spoke the word of God boldly.

Here Peter and John were in trouble for their outspokenness, and what did they do? They prayed for even a greater boldness! They had laid hold of Jesus' promise to them in Acts 1:8, "You shall receive power when the Holy Spirit has come upon you; and you shall be witnesses." Most of us get a severe attack of "chickenitis" when it comes to sharing the gospel, but we need to ask God for the power He has made available.

The hardest thing about sharing your faith with nonbelievers is getting started, forcing those first words out of your mouth. That's where the power of the Holy Spirit is essential. Once the ball is rolling, you'll discover that sharing your faith can become a joy, as well as a great blessing. Better yet, you may play an important role in the change of someone's eternal destiny.

Being Salt

Jesus concluded His own definition of discipleship in the gospel of Luke by saying, "Salt is good; but if the salt has lost its flavor, how shall it be seasoned?" (Luke 14:34). What did Jesus mean by this illustration? What is the "salt of the earth"?

To receive the full benefit of what Jesus was saying, we need to understand the first-century mindset. In Roman culture, salt was very important. Next to the sun, salt was the most important thing there was. Often, Roman soldiers were actually paid in salt, which is where the expression, "He's not worth his salt," comes from. With this in mind Jesus is saying, "You are to be salt in this earth. You are valuable. You can make a difference."

One very distinct quality of salt is that it affects everything it comes into contact with. Just a little salt in a glass of water can be tasted. In the same way, even one faithful Christian in an ungodly situation or place can make a difference!

Salt also stimulates thirst. Perhaps you can remember a time when you went to a movie theater and bought a box of popcorn. After you got to your seat and began to eat it, you became extremely thirsty because the attendant at the refreshment counter heavily salted it, knowing you would come back to buy a drink.

In the same way, if we live a godly life, it can stimulate a spiritual thirst in the lives of others to do likewise. If a nonbeliever sees something different in you, if he sees you are not like everyone else and you live a life directed by certain spiritual principles, he can find it very appealing. Many nonbelievers are also influenced when they see a Christian face severe circumstances and still maintain a sense of calmness and peace. Our lives are the only Bible many people will ever read. Christians are to be "living epistles," written by God and read by men.

One of the greatest compliments paid to a Christian is when a nonbeliever comes to him and says, "What is different about you? There's a quality that I admire, and I want to know more. Tell me about what you believe."

That is being salt! Smacking nonbelievers across the head with a Bible is not being a witness for Jesus. A more effective witness would be to let those nonbelievers around you watch and see the difference God has made in your life. Even something as subtle as taking your Bible to work and reading it quietly on your lunch hour could have a great impact.

Jesus has called us to be fishers of men, and one thing that is helpful in fulfilling that role is to first throw out the bait. If I'm aboard an airplane and want to start a conversation with the person next to me, I'll often pull out my Bible and set it on the tray. Some people look at me as if I had a highly contagious disease and want to quickly move. But there are others who will ask what I am reading. This often opens the door to share God's truth.

When you talk with someone about the Lord, it is generally a good idea to first share how God is working in your own life. Give the person an opportunity, and if he responds, "reel him in" a bit by telling him a little more about Jesus. If that individual's interest continues to grow, you can then explain what it means to know Christ, what Christ did, and what our response should be.

Sometimes the conversation will come to a point where the person doesn't want to hear anymore. Don't push it. The Bible says the servant of the Lord must not strive, but be gentle and patient with all men (2 Timothy 2:24,25). You can come to a point where a person has heard enough. That's the time to simply pull back and say, "If you want to know more, just read God's Word and I'll pray for you." I often recommend they read the Gospel of John, because it was written so that we may believe that Jesus was the Son of God (John 20:31). Then maybe that person will start the conversation up again.

The Bible says we are to be "wise as serpents and harmless as doves" (Matthew 10:16). We are to have wisdom without being overly aggressive. Some Christians try to stuff the gospel down people's throats. It will never work. Others use pressure, arguments, and coercion to get a person to come into the kingdom of God. I suppose they feel the end justifies the means. But keep this in mind. If someone can be argued into believing that person can also be argued out. If he can be pressured in, he can also be pressured out. Our responsibility as Christians is to proclaim the truth of the gospel and leave the converting up to God.

Being Light

Jesus used two analogies to show the impact

Christians should have in this world. We are to be salt and light. We have already seen what salt is. In contrast to salt, which is primarily *living* what you believe, light signifies *proclaiming* what you believe.

Jesus said, "Let your light so shine before men, that they may see your good works and glorify your Father in heaven" (Matthew 5:16). Too many believers try to be light without first being salt. They talk the Christian talk, but they don't live it. Quite honestly, it would have been better if they had not said a thing when they are not able to back it up with their lifestyle.

On the other side of the coin, there are those who are salt without being light. They live a godly life but don't tell people why! We must find the balance. The Scripture says in Romans 10:14, "How shall they believe in Him of whom they have not heard? And how shall they hear without a preacher?" God wants us to be the vehicle through which He can speak.

There is a right way and a wrong way to go "fishing for men." It is important to rely on Jesus and let Him guide us. I believe that God wants us to be sharp shooters, not machine gunners. I have seen machine-gun evangelists who gauge their success by how many people they can talk to in one hour. If you are doing that instead of really taking time with a person, it may not have any real or lasting effect. It may even drive people away.

I have found that the most effective sharing takes time. It is far better to sit down for an hour and talk deeply with one person than to peel off trite cliches to numbers of people. Some of the most profound things Jesus ever said were in one-on-one conversations. His talks with the woman at the well and with

Nicodemus have become our scripts for evangelism. He took time for these individuals. How much more should we!

We need to learn to let God's Holy Spirit lead us when sharing our faith. When a person comes to Christ, it will be a result of God's work, not our own. Jesus said, "No one can come to Me unless it has been granted to him by My Father" (John 6:65). No brilliant argument is going to win over another person. It must be the work of the Holy Spirit, and it must be in God's timing. That is why the Scripture tells us, "Preach the word! Be ready in season and out of season" (2 Timothy 4:2). Or, as another translation puts it, "Be on duty at all times." We need to always be ready. We never know when we will be called into action.

We Must Be Ready

Think of Philip, whom we read about in Acts 8:26-40. God simply told him to go to the desert. He didn't tell him that there would be a wealthy and powerful man from Ethiopia who would be searching for God and waiting for him when he arrived. He just said to go to the desert. Philip obeyed, and upon his arrival he found the man. His timing was just right. If Philip had lagged behind or run ahead, he would have missed out on the opportunity to lead this man to Christ.

Often we miss out on opportunities that God drops into our laps simply because we are not paying attention. Undoubtedly, God can get the job done without you or me. He will find someone else, but we will miss out on the privilege of being used by the Lord.

We can also learn a great deal from Philip's methods. He asked this Ethiopian an interesting question when he heard him reading from the writings of the prophet Isaiah. Philip asked, "Do you understand what you are reading?" And the Ethiopian responded by saying, "How can I unless someone shows me the way?"

Do you share your faith with others on a regular basis? If not, why? The evangelical magazine, *Christianity Today*, recently conducted a poll on why more believers do not share their faith. They asked whether churchgoers agreed or disagreed with some key statements. Among their findings:

+ 89% agreed or strongly agreed that faith in Christ was the only way to salvation.

+ 87% agreed or strongly agreed that every Christian is responsible for evangelism.

While not unanimous, more than half the respondents agreed or strongly agreed with the following:

+ I believe the most important task for Christians is to lead non-Christians to faith in Christ (68%).

+ I have been more active in telling others about Christ in the past year than ever before (52%).

And among the obstacles believers face in sharing their faith, the respondents listed the following as the biggest hurdles:

+ 49% feel unable to do evangelism as well as the professionals.

+ 43% said they were too timid.

✦ 40% said they were afraid of how people would respond.

Do We Care?

While I am sure many of us can relate to one or more of these obstacles, I think there is a deeper problem among many Christians today. If we were brutally honest, many of us would have to admit that we really don't care about the plight of the nonbeliever. In 1 Corinthians 9:16, the apostle Paul says, "For if I preach the gospel, I have nothing to boast of, for necessity is laid upon me; yes, woe is me if I do not preach the gospel!"

Evangelism must start with a genuine concern for the lost. The people we talk to can tell when we are sincere.

The apostle Paul had such a concern. He was so stirred for his own race to come to Christ that he said, "I have great sorrow and continual grief in my heart. For I could wish that I myself were accursed [or separated] from Christ for my brethren, my kinsmen according to the flesh" (Romans 9:2,3). Paul was saying he would be cut off himself if he could be confident that his countrymen would come to know Christ.

Moses had the same heart for Israel in the Old Testament. In Exodus 32, Moses went to Mount Sinai to receive the commandments of God. As the days passed and Moses still did not return to the camp, the people grew desperate and looked for a replacement for God in their lives. Under the misdirected leadership of Aaron, a golden calf was made and the people began to worship it.

As the sinful activity of the people was unfolding, God told Moses, "Go, get down! For your people whom you brought out of the land of Egypt have corrupted themselves."

The Lord then went on to speak about the guilt of the people, when Moses interrupted Him with the cry of prayer, "Lord, why does your wrath burn hot against Your people whom You have brought out of the land of Egypt with great power and with a mighty hand?"

"They are *your* people," God said to Moses.

"No, they are *your* people," Moses replied to God.

It is obvious that neither Moses or God wanted them in the condition they were in at that particular moment, naked and dancing around the golden calf. When Moses came down to the camp and saw this horrible spectacle of the people dancing naked around this graven image, he smashed the tablets God had given to him in righteous indignation.

The next day, Moses started back up the mountain with a great determination in his heart. When he reached the top, he began to speak to the Lord. As you will see, the statement that the burdened prophet made to the Lord is very significant. It is a sigh, a groan, a cry. It is a sentence that has no ending. Even in the King James Bible, the translators left the end of the sentence trailing, using a dash for punctuation. You might say it was a sentence that was broken in the middle by the sobs of a man who was asking to be sent to hell if only the people might be spared the righteous indignation of a holy God.

We read, "Then Moses returned unto the Lord, and said, 'Oh, these people have sinned a great sin, and have made for themselves a god of gold! Yet now, if you will forgive their sin—'"

At this point, the sentence stops and the translators end it with a dash. It must have been a long pause, for Moses was no doubt considering the full implications of what he was asking. He went on to pray, "But if not, I pray, blot me out of Your book which You have written."

As you can see, Moses was a man who had a tremendous burden for the people he was praying for, and he was willing to stand in the gap!

God, speaking of His desire to find people with such a burden, said, "So I sought for a man among them who would make a wall, and stand in the gap before Me on behalf of the land, that I should not destroy it; but I found no one" (Ezekiel 22:30).

The great Christian writer Alexander McClaren penned these words, "You tell me the depth of a Christian's compassion, and I will tell you the measure of his usefulness."

The Need to Be Flexible

In 1 Corinthians 9:20-23, Paul gives us a key to effectively sharing our faith. He writes, "And to the Jews I became as a Jew, that I might win Jews; to those who are under the law, as under the law, that I might win those who are under the law; to those who are without law, as without law (not being without law toward God, but under law toward Christ), that I might win those who are without law; to the weak I became as weak, that I might win the weak. I have become all things to all men, that I might by all means save some."

We could sum this aspect of evangelism up in one word: flexibility. You need to adapt yourself to other people. Jesus is our supreme example in this. Have you ever noticed that He never spoke to any two people in exactly the same way? He saw people as individuals. Some Christians share the great truths of the gospel as if it were coming off a Tele-type. They simply rattle off all of the information they have memorized. Memorizing Scripture, know-ing what you believe, and being able to present it effectively is right and good, but we also need to be sensitive to the people to whom we are speaking.

When Jesus talked to Pontius Pilate, the Roman leader asked him questions. Jesus responded to Pilate's interest. He spoke to Pilate about truth. But when Jesus was brought before Herod, He gave no answers. In Pilate, Jesus saw some genuine curi-osity; therefore, he responded accordingly. In con-trast, Jesus knew Herod had no genuine interest in spiritual things. He wanted to be dazzled, not changed. We, too, need to be discerning and not "cast our pearls before swine," offering the truths of God to someone who is not genuinely interested.

Jesus made these distinctions when He talked to other people as well. When Nicodemus came to Him and said, "No one can do the things you're doing unless He is from God," Jesus cut to the quick and said, "Look, Nicodemus, let's get down to brass tacks: You must be born again." He got right to the point. There are times when God will have us do the same. I've walked up to complete strangers and said, "Has anyone ever told you about Jesus Christ? I would like to share Him with you."

There have been other times, however, when I have felt it best not to take that approach. We see this with Jesus and the woman at the well. He sat down at a well as this woman came to draw water. She had come at noon because she was an outcast. This woman, as Jesus later pointed out, was di-vorced on a number of occasions, and was presently living with a man. Not only that, she was also a Samaritan.

In those days, Samaritans were looked down on by many of the Jews because of racial prejudice. Nevertheless, Jesus walked over to that well and sat down. As the woman was drawing water, Jesus asked, "Will you get me a drink?"

She turned and looked at Him in amazement, saying, "How is it that you, a Jew, would ask me, a Samaritan, for a drink?"

Then Jesus threw out a little bait by saying, "If you knew the gift of God and who it is that said to you 'give me a drink,' you would have asked of Him and He would have given you living water."

Having caught her interest, she then responded, "What is this living water you are talking about?"

There are times I have found this to work very well. In the course of a conversation with a nonbeliever, I might say, "I'm glad that God is in control of my life." That will usually get a little bit of reaction. One eyebrow goes up, they look at their watch, and perhaps go on their way as quickly as possible. Or they might say, "What do you mean, God is in control of your life?" These type of statements can act as bait to get attention. If they are interested, you can go a little further.

We Need Tact

I have often heard nonbelievers blast Christians for their lack of tact. Sometimes it ends up in name-calling, and the Christian goes away feeling he has been persecuted. But it is not persecution if that Christian has simply been irresponsible and insensitive in his methods of sharing Christ.

A good example of the right way to witness comes from the story of Philip and the Ethiopian eunuch we looked at earlier. The Ethiopian had come to Jerusalem searching for God, but sadly he did not find Him in the empty religion of that day. He did, however, pick up one very valuable item during his visit. He obtained a scroll containing the book of Isaiah. During his ride home, he was reading aloud from one of the great messianic chapters that speaks of Jesus, Isaiah 53.

At this time, God directed Philip to this powerful and wealthy, yet empty and searching, man. The way Philip approached him is a good illustration of using tact.

"Tact" is intuitively knowing how to say the right thing at the right time. (Unfortunately, some Christians have about as much tact as a bull in a china shop!) Philip simply said to this man, "Do you understand what you are reading?" He could have said, "Did you know that you are going to be judged by God and thrown into hell? What do you think about that?" Because Philip was sensitive to this man's need, he had an open door to share the gospel.

Love Is the Key

Another aspect of effective witnessing involves the heart. When Jesus came into contact with people, He genuinely loved them. He took an interest in them. Heartfelt concern will speak volumes to someone before you even utter a word. There are so very few people who really care anymore. Everyone seems to have ulterior motives—they want something from you. As a result, we have a world that is suspicious of anyone who talks with them. They think you must have a trick up your sleeve.

Once I was given two tickets to Disneyland. I was meeting some friends in the park, and I didn't need two tickets. I only needed one. As I walked in, I began to feel guilty that I was wasting one of these free admissions; after all, maybe there was someone who really wanted to go into the park but couldn't afford it. So I left the park and found some kids in the parking lot and offered the ticket to them. Their response was typical of everyone who has grown cynical about "free" offers: "What do you mean? Why are you giving me that ticket?" They didn't want it!

I approached a number of others before I finally found someone to take it. It took me nearly 30 minutes to convince someone there were no strings attached.

The world today is flooded with religious cults. Satan is no fool. He has put so many imitations out there that nonbelievers are suspicious of anyone who talks about God. These counterfeit Christians are in airports, malls, and streets in full force, sharing what they perceive to be the truth. We may not like what they are saying, or the way they are representing God, yet we must ask ourselves, "When was the last time I represented God?"

Jesus truly loved people, and we must do the same. That is our edge. The cults don't have Jesus' real love for people. We, however, have the same love as Jesus operating in our lives because the "love of God has been poured out in our hearts by the Holy Spirit" (Romans 5:5).

The Power of Personal Testimony

One of the most effective tools you can use in communicating your faith is your testimony (how you came to know Christ personally). If you go through the book of Acts and read some of the great evangelistic messages of the apostle Paul, you will find Paul often used his personal testimony. Certainly his was a dramatic one. But God can also use your personal testimony because it is unique.

Through your personal testimony, you can relay thoughts and feelings that other person can easily relate to. Having established that common ground, you can then share how God has worked in your life. In this way, you come back to the central message: Jesus Christ and Him crucified.

The Plan of Salvation

Once you have the opportunity to share the gospel, how exactly should you communicate it? It is important to point people to the Scriptures. But which ones should you share? Here is a plan of salvation from Scripture that you might want to memorize.

1. The Condition: We Are All Sinners

The first thing we need to establish with people is that they are sinners. People do not like this title. One word that defines sin is the Greek word *harmatia*, which means "to miss the mark." What is God's mark? Jesus said, "Be perfect . . . as your heavenly Father is perfect" (Matthew 5:48 NIV). Unless that person is perfect, they have missed the mark. Therefore, they are a sinner.

> 1 John 1:8,9: "If we say that we have no sin, we deceive ourselves, and the truth is not in us. If we confess our sins, He is faithful and just to forgive us our sins and to cleanse us from all unrighteousness."

> *Romans 3:23:* "All have sinned and fall short of the glory of God."

> *Isaiah 53:6:* "All we like sheep have gone astray; we have turned, every one, to his own way; and the Lord has laid on Him the iniquity of us all."

2. The Result: Death

Next, we need to establish, "What is the result of sin?"

> *Romans 6:23:* "The wages of sin is death."

Every one of us has missed God's mark. Every one of us has fallen short of being perfect. The result of that is death. We are getting only what we deserve, and we are bringing that judgment upon ourselves. One thing we all need to remember is that God does not send anyone to hell. We send ourselves there by rejecting His truth.

3. The Solution: Christ's Death on the Cross

At this point, let people know the solution: Christ died for our sins.

> *John 3:16,17:* "For God so loved the world that He gave His only begotten Son, that whoever believes in Him should not perish but have everlasting life. For God did not send His Son into the world to condemn the world, but that the world through Him might be saved."

> *Isaiah 53:5:* "He was wounded for our transgressions, He was bruised for our iniquities."

> *Romans 5:8:* "God demonstrates His own love toward us, in that while we were still sinners, Christ died for us."

Since we can never measure up to God's standards on our own, God has reached out to man. We cannot solve the problem of sin, but God, who is perfect, can and has. He has become a bridge for us through Jesus Christ.

4. The Choice: To Accept or Reject Jesus Christ as Savior

If a person will acknowledge that he is a sinner, and he accepts the premise that Christ is the solution, he is at a crossroads. Either he can reject God's solution and accept the consequences, or he can accept Jesus Christ as his Savior. What must a person do to to be forgiven of his sins and come into a relationship with God?

First, that person must repent.

> *Luke 13:3:* "I tell you . . . unless you repent you will all likewise perish."
>
> *Acts 3:19:* "Repent therefore and be converted, that your sins may be blotted out, so that times of refreshing may come from the presence of the Lord."
>
> *Acts 17:30:* "These times of ignorance God overlooked, but now commands all men everywhere to repent."

Once a person has realized that he is a sinner and has repented of that sin, he must come to Jesus Christ.

> *Matthew 11:28-30:* "Come to Me, all you who labor and are heavy laden, and I will give you rest. Take My yoke upon you and learn from Me, for I am gentle and lowly in heart, and you will find rest for your souls. For My yoke is easy and My burden is light."

5. *The Response: To Receive the Gift of Eternal Life*

Christ's invitation is clear. We must come to Him. All that remains is a response.

> *Romans 6:23:* "The gift of God is eternal life in Christ Jesus our Lord."

What must we do to receive that gift? Take it!

> *Revelation 3:20:* "Behold, I stand at the door and knock. If anyone hears My voice and opens the door, I will come in to him and dine with him, and he with Me."

Jesus stands at the door of your heart and mine and knocks, seeking entrance into our lives. What do we have to do to let Him come in? Open the door!

> *John 1:12:* "But as many as received Him, to them He gave the right to become children of God."

We must receive Him. How? By asking Him into our lives. If we have shared these truths to a non-believer, and that person wants to receive Christ, then we need only ask him to do it. In fact, we should pray with him at that very moment if he would like to make this life-changing decision to receive and follow Jesus Christ. I know of no greater joy than leading someone in a prayer to receive Christ.

6. *The Assurance of Salvation*

Following this, it is important that the new believer has assurance that Christ has come into his life.

1 John 5:11-13: "This is the testimony: that God has given us eternal life, and this life is in His Son. He who has the Son has life; he who does not have the Son of God does not have life. These things I have written to you who believe in the name of the Son of God, that you may know that you have eternal life, and that you may continue to believe in the name of the Son of God."

2 Corinthians 5:17: "Therefore, if anyone is in Christ, he is a new creation; old things have passed away; behold, all things have become new."

Psalm 103:12: "As far as the east is from the west, so far has He removed our transgressions from us."

7. The Profession of Faith

At this time, you may encourage the new believer to make a public confession of his newfound faith in Christ.

> *Matthew 10:32,33:* "Therefore whoever confesses Me before men, him I will also confess before My Father who is in heaven. But whoever denies Me before men, him I will also deny before My Father who is in heaven."

After you have led someone to Christ, it is important to take the new Christian under your wing and help him get established in his relationship with Christ.

Discipling a New Believer

The full concept of discipleship is to share our faith, lead people to Christ, and then to help them mature. But somewhere along the line we have separated evangelism from discipleship. There is no such distinction in Scripture. The idea is not to just pray with someone and say, "See you later. God bless you." It is to help that believer to grow spiritually and become a dedicated, committed, fruitful, and mature disciple of Jesus Christ. Then we trust that believer will repeat the process with someone else. And so the cycle continues.

After Saul's conversion, there was great doubt among the believers as to whether he'd had a true conversion. Saul was one of the prime persecutors of the early church. He presided over the first execution of a Christian in the New Testament, a young man named Stephen. Upon hearing that the notorious Saul had become a believer, the disciples were afraid it was just a ploy to find out where they met so he could turn them over to the authorities. But God spoke to a man named Ananias and said, "I want you to go and visit Saul. He is your brother and he is in prayer." Ananias obeyed, found Saul (who later changed his name to Paul), and took the time to pray for him and encourage him.

Then God brought another man into Paul's life named Barnabas. Barnabas introduced Paul to the apostles and personally reassured them that his conversion was sincere.

This is a good illustration of true discipleship. Discipling someone is not just teaching that person: it's also being a friend to that individual. Tragically, I find that many people who first accept Christ often fall through the cracks because no one helps them become established in the faith. It can be difficult for these people to get acclimated to church.

A new believer may come to church for the first time and see everyone having wonderful fellowship, but then when the Bible study starts and the pastor says, "Turn to Matthew 5, verse 3," he feels lost because he hasn't the faintest idea where to look.

That is exactly how I felt when I first came to church. I remember how I didn't understand the language of the Christians. They had there own unique vocabulary. You might even call it "Christianese." I thank God that a believer saw me and took me under his wing. He invited me to church and introduced me to his Christian friends. After the services, he explained what different things meant and answered my questions.

One couple in Scripture, Aquila and Priscilla, illustrate how we should help new converts. They saw a young man named Apollos who was filled with enthusiasm for the Lord. However, he needed more insight into what he was teaching. Aquila and Priscilla took him into their home and "explained to him the way of God more accurately" (Acts 18:26). As a result, Apollos became even more effective in what God had called him to do.

When we lead someone to Christ, or meet a new convert, we must take the initiative to see that he is stabilized in his newfound faith. As I already stated, you need to take that person to church with you, introduce him to your friends, and, most importantly, be a friend.

A new believer not only needs to hear the truth; he needs to see it lived. He can't get that from a pulpit. He needs to see it in a lifestyle. Obviously, he will have many questions! How does a Christian act at work? How does a Christian behave when he drives? How does a Christian treat his wife and children? How does a Christian spend his free time? What movies does a Christian see? These are all a part of the discipleship process.

A mature believer can be a model for applying the truths of God. Colossians 1:28 says, "Him we preach, warning every man and teaching every man in all wisdom, that we may present every man perfect in Christ Jesus."

The Scripture is full of examples of this discipling process. The apostle Paul repeated the discipling process he had gone through with young Timothy. Elijah discipled Elisha. Moses discipled Joshua. And most notably, Jesus discipled His disciples. In speaking of this process, Paul said in 1 Thessalonians 2:11, "For you know that we dealt with each of you as a father deals with his own children, encouraging, comforting and urging you to live lives worthy of God" (NIV).

One thing that keeps Christians from being active disciples is the fear of not having sufficient Bible knowledge. It is not necessary that you be a Bible scholar to lead someone to Christ and disciple them. Remember, you probably know a lot more than a brand-new believer knows. You can begin by sharing the building blocks of the Christian life that this book talks about: how to pray; how to read the Bible; how to get the most out of church; and how to live a godly life. Your life can impact that person's life in a wonderful way.

Benefits of Discipling

This last building block—the discipling of others—is an extremely important one. The failure to make disciples will have damaging results on your own walk with Christ. Attending more Bible studies, more prayer meetings, reading more Christian books, listening to more teaching tapes without an outlet for the truth we acquire will cause us to spiritually decay. We need to take what God has given us and use it constructively in the lives of others.

When taking a new believer under your wing, you are not only encouraging a new child of God, but you are saving yourself from spiritual stagnation. The new believer needs our wisdom, knowledge, and experience, and we need the zeal, spark, and childlike simplicity of faith that a young Christian possesses.

Have you ever led anyone to Jesus Christ? Have you discipled anyone? Have you taken any new believer under your wing and helped him along? If you will, it will reignite *your* spiritual life as that person discovers the truths of God for the first time and you rediscover them.

Children are the best illustration of this process. When you are with a child, you begin to see things through a child's eyes again. As the child discovers things for the first time, you rediscover the newness of those things. It is wonderful when a child first discovers the ocean, walks on sand, picks up snow, or tastes ice cream. These are things we adults take for granted, but when we see a child discover them, we share in his excitement.

In the same way, when we see a new believer discover things from the Word and the excitement it brings, it reignites us. Often, they will ask difficult questions that will make us search the Scriptures for answers. And there are always things we have learned but forgotten. A new believer's questions can help us to rediscover (or discover for the first time) many important spiritual truths.

The fact is, many mature Christians come to a point where they simply dry up. When this happens, many begin wondering what is wrong with them. Some seek a solution in finding a new church, or some new teaching that supposedly will revolutionize their lives. In most cases, the real problem is simply spiritual sluggishness. The person in this position should be passing along what he has learned to a younger believer.

Jesus said that "whoever has [or is passing it on], to him more will be given, and he will have abundance; but whoever does not have [is not passing it on], even what he has will be taken away from him" (Matthew 13:12).

Proverbs 11:25 says, "The generous soul will be made rich, and he who waters will also be watered himself." I have found that the more I give, the more God seems to give back to me.

At one point the children of Israel were facing the problem of spiritual stagnation. God told them through the prophet Isaiah to get their eyes off of their own problems and start giving away what they had been given. Isaiah 58:6 says, "Is this not the fast that I have chosen: to loose the bonds of wickedness, to undo the heavy burdens, to let the oppressed go free, and that you break every yoke?"

His promise to them for being obedient is found shortly thereafter in Isaiah 58:8, "Then your light shall break forth like the morning, your healing shall spring forth speedily."

You can be a partaker of that same promise if you will open up your life to disciple someone else! It can start today, right where you are and with the people God has brought into your life. For the sake of those who don't yet know Christ, don't forsake God's command to "go and make disciples." For the sake of a young believer, don't let apathy rob you of being a blessing to him or her. And for the sake of maintaining an exciting, fruitful walk with God, don't ignore these commands of Jesus. The promises and the blessings are for those who will apply these principles. Indeed, the harvest is plenteous and the laborers are few. We need more laborers, more disciples. May God help you and me to be just that!

Remember, it "takes one to make one." I hope the simple principles I have outlined in this book will help you to better understand what it means to be a true disciple of Jesus Christ, and that you might experience *radical Christian living* for yourself.